The COMPETITION–COOPERATION Link

Games for Developing Respectful Competitors

Daniel W. Midura, MEd

Roseville Area Schools
Roseville, Minnesota

Donald R. Glover, MS

White Bear Lake Area Public Schools
White Bear Lake, Minnesota

Human Kinetics

Library of Congress Cataloging-in-Publication Data

Midura, Daniel W., 1948-
    The competition–cooperation link: games for developing respectful
competitors / by Daniel W. Midura and Donald R. Glover.
      p. cm.
    Includes bibliographical references (p. 145).
    ISBN 0-88011-850-4
    1. Physical education and training. 2. Physical education and
training--Psychological aspects. 3. Cooperativeness.
4. Competition (Psychology) in youth. 5. Group games. I. Glover,
Donald R. II. Title.
GV362.M486   1998
613.7'07—DC21   98-22391
                                                  CIP

GV
362
.M486
1999

ISBN: 0-88011-850-4

Acquisitions Editor: Scott Wikgren; **Developmental Editor:** Lynn M. Hooper-Davenport; **Managing Editor:** Melinda Graham; **Assistant Editors:** Jennifer Goldberg and Jennifer Miller; **Copyeditor:** Judy Peterson; **Proofreader:** Erin Cler; **Graphic Designer:** Nancy Rasmus; **Graphic Artist:** Francine Hamerski; **Photo Editor:** Boyd LaFoon; **Cover Designer:** Keith Blomberg; **Photographer (cover):** Tom Roberts; **Photographer (interior):** Don Glover, except where otherwise noted; **Illustrators:** Tom Roberts, Mac art; Susan Carson, line art; **Printer:** United Graphics

Printed in the United States of America   10 9 8 7 6 5 4 3 2 1

Human Kinetics
Web site: http://www.humankinetics.com/

United States: Human Kinetics, P.O. Box 5076, Champaign, IL 61825-5076
1-800-747-4457
e-mail: humank@hkusa.com

Canada: Human Kinetics, 475 Devonshire Road Unit 100, Windsor, ON N8Y 2L5
1-800-465-7301 (in Canada only)
e-mail: humank@hkcanada.com

Europe: Human Kinetics, P.O. Box IW14, Leeds LS16 6TR, United Kingdom
(44) 1132 781708
e-mail: humank@hkeurope.com

Australia: Human Kinetics, 57A Price Avenue, Lower Mitcham, South Australia 5062
(088) 277 1555
e-mail: humank@hkaustralia.com

New Zealand: Human Kinetics, P.O. Box 105-231, Auckland 1
(09) 523 3462
e-mail: humank@hknewz.com

To Shirley, Luke, and Seth. Thanks for being so supportive of my work. You are the joys of my life. Luke and Seth, you have become all the things I cherish in good, respectful competitors.

Dan Midura

To my grandchildren, Jessie, Alexa, and Jacob, in hopes that they will learn to become respectful competitors.

Don Glover

CONTENTS

ACTIVITY FINDER

Activity	Duration	Page	Objective
Last Runner Out	5-10 minutes	42	Helps students control their running pace.
First Runner to the Back	5-10 minutes	44	Reinforces the concepts of pacing, baton passing, and provides a controlled warm-up.
Rip Flag Scramble	5-10 minutes	47	Incorporates running, dodging, changing directions, and grasping.
Fastest Tag in the World	5-10 minutes	50	Provides a vigorous warm-up game that incorporates running, dodging, changing directions, stopping, and safe tagging.
EDW 500	5-10 minutes	52	Combines running and a variety of designated training activities.
Rip-Off Champ	5-10 minutes	55	Reinforces skills of running, dodging, changing directions, spatial awareness, agility, and body control.
Color Tag	15-30 minutes	57	Reinforces skills of running, dodging, changing directions, and safe tagging.
Encyclopedia Tag	15-30 minutes	60	Reinforces skills of running, dodging, changing directions, and safe tagging.
Frozen Tag	15-30 minutes	63	Emphasizes skills of running, changing directions, dodging, agility, body control, and spatial awareness.

PREFACE

The physical education profession is currently embroiled in vigorous debate regarding the place competitive activities have in our educational curriculum. To many, competition is looked upon as the antithesis to cooperative learning. To these people, competition, once viewed as a vital element of physical education, has become a bad word. Certainly, as physical education teachers, we could eliminate many or all competitive activities from our curriculum. However, countless young people who enter the world of youth or community athletic programs will be facing the elements of competition directly. We believe that a physical education program is the most encompassing vehicle for teaching students how to cooperate and compete effectively and enjoyably in physical activity settings. We further believe that by this teaching, we are not only preparing students to enjoy physical activity for a lifetime, but we are also helping prepare children to be successful in the workplace, to enjoy personal relationships, and to perhaps some day be good parents and even good volunteer coaches and youth leaders.

In preparing to write this book, we were struck by the diverse opinions people have regarding competition and cooperation. To some, competition is what made America great; they feel that today's emphasis on cooperation could cause us to lose our competitive edge in the world trade market.

To others, competition is evil and the primary reason people reject physical activity, which consequently leads to the sedentary lifestyle of many Americans. Physical educators adhering to the anticompetition philosophy believe that overemphasizing competition causes many students to withdraw from physical activity. They believe it is cooperation that is most successful in helping all students prepare to be physically active for a lifetime and to be better team players in the workplace.

What people on both sides of this debate fail to realize is that neither competition nor cooperation is inherently good or evil. It is how we deal with competition and cooperation that can allow for effective or ineffective results. For example, for every incident you find of a child having a positive experience in youth sport, you can find a child having a negative experience in youth sport. Upon closer examination, you will find that it was a coach, parent, or official who caused the youth sport experience to be either positive or negative for the child.

Throughout our lives, we will face circumstances that require cooperation, a combination of cooperation and competition, or competition. Therefore, it is our task as teachers to prepare our students to successfully, effectively, and responsibly face these circumstances. The purpose of this book is to help put respect and cooperation into competition, and to clearly show the role that team building plays in the physical education curriculum. In addition, we have included 30 activities, which are explained in great detail; they can be used to help you teach the concepts that enhance the link between competition and cooperation.

Before moving into the activities, we provide an overview of cooperation and competition. In chapter 1, we define terms and outline the complex relationship between cooperation and competition. In chapter 2, we present ways to integrate competition and cooperation at different age levels. In chapter 3, we outline a sample program on how to incorporate cooperative skills into a class. Chapter 4 describes ways to reinforce healthy attitudes and expectations, and we offer criteria for selecting activities that can be used to teach effective cooperative and competitive activities.

In chapter 5, we present activities that have been carefully designed to provide a link between competition and cooperation. Most active adults can play a highly competitive game of tennis, racquetball, or golf with a friend and still enjoy their friendship. We believe we can help our students learn to do this through carefully constructed activities.

It is imperative that physical educators not only teach students about wellness and instill in them an appreciation and enjoyment of lifetime physical activities, but also that we create in our students an appreciation and understanding of how to be a good competitor and a good teammate, and put competition into a balanced perspective. We hope you will find this book to be a valuable tool in designing a physical education program that can accomplish these goals.

ACKNOWLEDGMENTS

We wish to thank Leigh Anderson, the sixth-grade teacher whose team building work is featured in chapter 3 of this book. Mrs. Anderson, who teaches at Heritage Middle School in West St. Paul, Minnesota, has embraced team building by developing a classroom–gym partnership that enhances and promotes social skills. Her Master's thesis presents an in-depth review of team building and was very useful to us as we wrote chapters 1 and 3 of this book.

Thanks also to Debbie Vigil, for her contributions to chapter 3, and to Lorri Bettenga, for her photography work. We also thank our developmental editor at Human Kinetics, Lynn Hooper-Davenport, as well as our acquisitions editor, Scott Wikgren, for their support of this project.

INTRODUCTION

In our books, *Team Building Through Physical Challenges* and *More Team Building Challenges*, we set out to create activities that, by their very nature, would direct students into situations that required them to work together for the good of a group. We dealt with the subjects of creating success experiences, allowing for failure to occur during tasks, and persevering so that a group could accomplish success. Additionally, we set out to show that we can teach students to be positive and to reduce or eliminate negative pressures and put-downs toward one another, and to handle failure with an attitude that failure can be a step toward success, not an end in itself. We also feel that one of the greatest services we can provide our students is to teach them to be accountable for their actions and responses. By providing clear and specific expectations we then are able to provide clear and specific consequences for not following those expectations. Students doing our team building activities are required to pay a sacrifice for breaking the stated expectations. The sacrifice usually is a big price to pay.

The response we have received to our team building activities has been exciting and overwhelming. Wherever we have gone, educators have embraced the activities as being not only fun and motivating but educationally sound.

It has never been our intent to set team building activities against other physical education activities. We are in no way against competition, nor do we feel that team building activities should replace all games and motor skill activities. On the contrary, we have deeply felt that team building activities should supplement the physical education program and be used as a tool to equip our students with the skills to make them better students, friends, and more creative people.

But how do we link team building and competition? We personally want our students to enjoy all types of physical activity, including competitive games. It is our desire to see our students enjoying not only the games they play but also enjoying their teammates and opponents. We want our students to recognize that losing a volleyball game 16–14 can be much more fun than winning 15–1. Why not teach our students that they can play a competitive game of tennis, racquetball, or golf with a friend, play their hearts out, and still enjoy the friendship?

Most of the 30 activities in this book are designed so that students are working cooperatively with small groups or partners. Some of the activities have a competitive nature, yet include a focus on the qualities of respect and recognition of teamwork. None of the lessons will guarantee the desired outcome unless the instructor has a commitment to teach to that outcome. Few activities, by their nature, create within students a desire to help one another and show respect for others or create a spirit of placing others before oneself.

The activities provided in this book link team building characteristics to activities that are competitive in their design. However, saying an activity is a cooperative activity doesn't guarantee it to be so. We must demand and expect specific responses to the activities we teach. If we want students to exhibit polite behavior, we must demonstrate the behavior, reinforce the behavior, model the behavior, give plenty of practice using the behavior, and correct incorrect responses when they occur. We should expect some wrong responses and not allow them to diminish our resolve to correct and teach the right behavior.

Team building teaches children to recognize negative behaviors, behaviors that may cause a group to fail. In fact, if just one person uses a negative behavior, the entire group may fail. Negative pressures and put-downs are two of the worst enemies of cooperative group behavior and healthy competition. Children need to be taught to eliminate these behaviors from their team.

Positive behaviors must be reinforced. Behaviors such as listening to others, encouraging teammates, praising teammates' efforts, and appreciating the efforts of others are actions that need to be learned. At a young age, praising another person's effort can be difficult. One reason children find this an awkward skill is because they do not practice it. We teach many physical skills. Teaching children to praise is just as important as teaching any physical skill.

Teaching children to respect one another is so very important. If we put kids into competitive situations too early, or put them into a program with an unknowing coach, our efforts at building respectful competitors will fail.

The activities and lessons in this book are designed to make the link between team building and competitive activities a simple and smooth one.

Part I
Teaching Strategies

Photo by Lorri Bettenga

Chapter 1

UNDERSTANDING COMPETITION AND COOPERATION

Photo by Lorri Bettenga

Large scale success is spelled t-e-a-m-w-o-r-k. Successful team workers don't wear a chip on their shoulder, don't look for slights, and they put the good of the company or team first. And if the team prospers, individuals, as active, effective, and progressive parts of it, will prosper too.

B.C. Forbes
American publisher, as quoted in *The Edge*

When children are toddlers and preschoolers, they learn about the world through curiosity and movement. Children of this age often engage in creative and imaginative play. As children grow, the type of play may change, but the purpose of play remains: children play because it is fun. Children have fun competing at very young ages but winning or losing does not seem to be a very important part of their play. As children grow, however, many find that as they compete others in their environment or social groups are placing more emphasis on winning and losing. Furthermore, because adults tend to define competition in terms of winning and losing, as they get more involved in the children's activities they may pressure the children to play to win. The pleasure of playing for fun can begin to fade. Then, when these same adults see the pressure and resulting stress experienced by the children, many blame competition itself for the results.

Because we have written two books about teamwork and its value to individuals and to society, some may have assumed that we feel competition is harmful. That certainly is not the case. In our opinion competition is neither inherently good nor bad. We feel competition simply means that an individual or group of individuals (a team) is trying to achieve a goal by comparing one performance to that of another individual or team.

Other people tend to regard competition as either highly desirable or very destructive. Thus, to some, competition is natural, healthy, and essential for building character. They view it as a valuable means to socialize children, as a significant force in motivating behavior, and, to many, as highly enjoyable. To others, competition is regarded as harmful, psychologically damaging, and detrimental to cooperative activity while, conversely, cooperative activity is endowed with all manner of beneficial effects and is seen as the highest state of human relations. One researcher has declared that competition is destructive, irrational, and highly counterproductive (Sherif 1976).

The charge is often made that competition teaches young people to be violent and aggressive. We probably all can find illustrations to support that argument. We might agree that aggression can easily turn into violent behavior. Professional hockey is frequently used as an example of how competition fosters violent behavior. Observers of professional hockey note that severe penalties, assessed for rule infractions or loss of control, often do not effectively deter those behaviors from being repeated. In fact, the fighting among professional hockey players does not result from a loss of restraint or self-control, but rather is a behavior encouraged by those promoting the sport. Fighting sells tickets, they believe. People will pay to see the behavior. On the other hand, the game can be played without the violent behavior. Olympic hockey, which has very little fighting, is played as the game should be: as a highly skilled game of skating, passing, and stick handling.

How do we encourage competition, yet minimize aggression? How do we effectively teach that participation in competitive activities should lead to sportsmanship, discipline, and control? We find that anxiety and frustration are emotions that can be controlled if we take time to teach young athletes not only to control these emotions but to react positively to opponents as well as teammates.

Violence in schools is increasing. Although critics have expressed opposing views, we believe that learning to become a better teammate by becoming more tolerant of others and by following and accepting rules of play, gives hope that violent behavior can be reduced. In our opinion, competition can be both productive and counterproductive. So where does one cross the line in this debate (or argument)? Adults and role models can determine the effects of competition on a child. We do not believe competition is harmful, but we do believe that the attitudes adults bring to the young persons' activities often determine whether the competition is productive.

Many teachers support our position. We received a letter from Moreland Public School in West St. Paul, Minnesota that reads: "Thank you so much for the team building ideas and activities. We have been doing team building with our sixth grade students here at Moreland. All the sixth grade teachers have noticed quite a difference in attitudes and behaviors. Quarreling after physical education and competitive activities has diminished." You may not experience quarreling among your students as a result of your activities, but team building can help to change their attitudes toward competition and, consequently, toward their teammates.

Despite the belief by some people that competitive sport is harmful to children, one thing is very clear—competition is a very big part of our children's lives and it will be here for a long time. A simple observation of the financial force of youth sports bears witness to the likely continuation of competitive events. Little league sports of every type are growing in popularity and participants. There are more opportunities today than ever before for children to participate in organized sport. As a result, it is more important than ever that we better understand competition and how it affects our children. We also have to understand cooperation and teamwork and how these ideas mesh with one another.

Let's start by taking a close look at competition.

WHAT IS COMPETITION?

As stated previously, competition is a process of comparing skills. An individual or a team is trying to achieve a goal by outperforming another individual or team. There doesn't seem to be anything wrong with this; in fact, it sounds to many like fun. However, within the confines of this definition, there are different types of competition, some of which could be, if administered by an influential adult, detrimental to a child's emotional development. Martin Ralbovosky, in 1974, wrote: "Adult-corrupted activities teach kids how to fight and cheat, they exclude those who could benefit most, and they cripple and maim the young in pursuit of victory." It would seem that Mr. Ralbovosky is not in favor of competitive activities for children. Yet, can they be as bad as he says? We will examine several models of competition.

Military Model

In the military model of competition, the opponent is regarded as the enemy. The military model is characterized by obsessive ranking of teams and individuals according to playing statistics. Derisive relationships often exist among coaches, players, and parents. The language of competition is laden with military terms and concepts: a quarterback's arm is his weapon, opponents are to be feared and defeated, teams battle for honor (Runfola and Sabo 1980). Actually, isn't this a picture of the daily newspaper's sports pages?

Many who endorse the military view of competition would frown on being friendly with one's opponents. Personally, we do not think the military model of competition administered by an authoritarian coach or teacher is best for children.

Reward Model

Many researchers and scholars who have studied competition, including Alfie Kohn, define competition by the reward one strives to attain. In Kohn's model of competition, everyone competes for the same reason—winning. He assumes that everyone competing does so in order to best the other competitors. Kohn seems to believe that the central message of all competition is that other people should be looked at as hazards or objects getting in the way of our success.

When something other than winning becomes the goal or reward, the reward model of competition is inadequate because each team, indeed every individual, may have a separate goal. Thus, each person or team may have a different definition of the reward in the contest. For example, athletes often enjoy playing skilled competitors because it will help to raise their own skill level. You may love playing one-on-one against an all-state guard on your basketball team knowing you will not beat that person, but you enjoy playing that guard because you will improve your game or skills. You look at that person not as an object getting in the way of your success but as a means of contributing to your success.

Another example of a goal other than winning is the desire to achieve a certain level of performance. Consider yourself an average tennis player who has been given an opportunity to play a professional. It is obvious you cannot win the game, and your goal is not to do so. You decide to set as your goal scoring a certain number of points, returning a certain number of serves, or returning a certain percentage of serves. Your goal will probably be very different from your opponent's. Thus, defining competition on the basis of rewards or winning makes little sense because the rewards are subjectively determined (Martens 1977).

Partnership Model

In contrast to the military and reward models of competition, the partnership model emphasizes that teammates, coaches, and opposing players view each other as comrades rather than enemies (Anderson 1996). Players with disparate ability levels are respected and treated as peers rather than ranked in a hierarchy, and athletes care for each other as well as themselves. The word "compete" is derived from the Latin *competere*, to seek together (Nelson 1991). Thus, the partnership model describes a compassionate, egalitarian approach to sport in which athletes are motivated by love of themselves, of sports, and of each other. Power is understood not as power *over* (power as dominance) but as power *to* (power as competence) (Anderson 1996). Like early physical educators, partnership athletes maintain that sport should be inclusive, in balance with other aspects of life, cooperative and social in spirit, and safe (Oglesby 1989).

Mariah Nelson (1991) gives the following specific examples describing the partnership theory of competition. Chris Evert and Martina Navratilova established a 14-year friendship and rivalry in tennis that symbolizes the partnership model of competition. Navratilova has explained that she is different from athletes who believe you have to hate your opponent in order to reach the top. She says she personally couldn't understand that. For her, playing hard and being able to go to dinner with her opponent afterward was greatly rewarding. Jackie Joyner-Kersee says, "I don't need to be enemies with someone in order to compete against them." Lauren Crux and Tish Denevan are competitors in body surfing. From spring through fall they surf together weekly, then compete against each other on weekends. They watch out for each other when one gets dumped, applaud successes, and share new tricks. "Next to the surfing itself, the camaraderie is the greatest joy," says Lauren. "The beginners will be there, and Tish and I will be there; the joy is having people laughing and playing, truly thrilled."

This sounds more like the type of competition in which the majority of parents and children would like to engage. Perhaps this is the model we should bring to school-age children.

Undoubtedly, the various approaches to competition will continue to evoke considerable controversy. However, with escalating sport participation and increased fascination with sports, it is naive to think competition will be eliminated from physical education or athletics. Therefore, the issue is not whether competition should exist in youth athletics, but rather how to increase the likelihood that competition benefits the individual (Dubois 1980). We think this can be done by linking cooperation to competition.

WHAT IS COOPERATION?

Webster's dictionary defines cooperation as "working together willingly to achieve a common purpose. " This certainly sounds like teamwork; good teamwork or effective cooperation is an essential foundation of a competitive team. Can cooperation be the ally of competition? There are plenty of authors and scholars who certainly favor one side of the debate over the other.

In *Cooperative Sports and Games Book,* Terry Orlick (1978) stresses cooperative games over competition. Play and games continually involve people in the areas of acting, reacting, feeling, and experiencing. Cooperative play brings people together to learn and have fun at the same time. However, if you distort children's play by rewarding excessive competition and physical aggression toward others, you often encourage cheating, unfair play, feelings of frustration, defeat, and isolation. Few, if any, would appreciate this result.

The concept behind cooperative play or teamwork is simple: people play with one another to overcome challenges, not to overcome other people. No player is excluded or banished to warm the bench and nurse a bruised self-image, as so often happens in competitive activities. Since success depends upon completing challenges, children are channeled into cooperating with one another. Children play together while learning how to become more considerate of one another, they are more aware of others' feelings and begin to look for the contributions each teammate can offer the team (Orlick 1978). Is it possible that these same qualities of cooperative play can be incorporated onto a team in a competitive situation? While it is true that a competitive team may be trying to overcome another team, it is still important that the individuals on the team learn these cooperative principles in order to benefit the entire team.

Orlick (1978) has found through his studies that well-designed cooperative game programs consistently show an increase in cooperative behavior in games, in free play, and in the classroom for the children involved in these programs. One of the many positive results of these programs is for children to be more receptive to sharing both human and material resources. Orlick explains, "The change does not occur overnight, but rather, over a period of several months the children seem to become more considerate and caring individuals." Ideas, talents, concerns, feelings, respect, possessions, equipment, time, space, and responsibility become recognizable by the students, and desirable qualities to possess.

It seems that the underlying appeal of teamwork lies in its ability to create a sense of community or a feeling of belonging. No one is left out. The feelings of children can be summed up by a student who said, "I felt left in," as he referred to cooperative games (Orlick 1978).

In *Everyone Wins,* Sambhava Luvmour (1979) describes situations in which creating a sense of belonging through teamwork or cooperation have proven successful. For example, the students at an elementary school were playing competitive games during recess and having a great deal of problems as a result. Conflicts began, students started fighting, formed cliques, and escalated these activities when the adults intervened. Playground supervisors were frustrated with lack of support, and the parents blamed other parents, children, and teachers. A solution was desperately needed. Cooperative games were introduced as the hopeful answer and they proved to be successful. Adult supervisors were trained to teach these games, and more games were introduced in physical education classes. Children began to channel their energies into cooperative activities rather than just competing against one another. Playing for fun helped to eliminate the fighting, cheating, put-downs, and name calling that were so common in the games played for the purpose of winning or beating your opponent.

We contend that in learning the importance of being a good team member, a person is learning a significant lifetime skill. If the number one skill desired by the Fortune 500 companies is the ability to work as part of a team, then sports and cooperative games are significantly valuable in teaching this concept and skill. More young people are involved in organized sports than in any other recreational interest. Imagine the benefits to these young people of learning the value of fun and teamwork over the need to win. They would not only be learning physical skills that are essential for maintaining a healthy lifestyle but also extremely important social skills.

Coaches and parents have a wonderful opportunity to help our children develop into happy, healthy human beings. The adults can spend less time on competitive strategies and competitive intensity at the young ages and more time on teaching kids to be good teammates. Children should be taught the characteristics of being a good teammate. We do not have to chastise, scold, or embarrass them because they don't know the Xs and Os of their sport. Knowledge of the game will come with experience. Cooperation and teamwork should be taught first.

Chapter 2

INTEGRATING COOPERATION AND COMPETITION

Try to forget yourself in the service of others. For when we think too much of ourselves and our own interests, we easily become despondent. But, when we work for others, our efforts return to bless us.

Sydney Powell
American clergyman, as quoted in *The Edge*

Competition can be fun and healthy if we, as parents and teachers, instruct kids how to cooperate within the confines of a team and provide activities and social skills that lead to healthy attitudes about competition. Competition can lead to many positive rewards. Yet if we simply instruct children to win, praise the winners, and pressure the losers to improve their performance, then children connect self-worth to winning and losing—competition can then become destructive.

We believe team building and cooperative activities can make competition more fun and rewarding. Team building does this by encouraging positive behavior and by putting the focus on the team interaction rather than on the end result. One of the most important lessons of team building is that losing, or failure, is only temporary. If the team reorganizes, practices, and perseveres, then success can be achieved, and it is much sweeter. Isn't this a lesson that all children should learn, the value of perseverance?

When we link team building to physical education, we must make sure our children and students participate in programs that will not only enhance their physical skills but also seriously promote social and emotional development. We need to look for programs that provide the following elements:

1. A sound teaching or coaching philosophy, a philosophy that provides participation for everyone.
2. A strong educational program for coaches. Coaches who preach the doctrine of "win at all costs" should be avoided. Exemplary physical educators, recreational directors, and coaches need to educate their players and the players' parents in the joys of the activity being taught and played, reinforce their players to eliminate the pressure to win, and reinforce their players in their encouragement of one another.
3. Ways to equalize teams so that everyone has the chance to experience some success.
4. Instructions in skill acquisition not just competition.

We believe that quality, competitive programs cannot be possible without quality teachers and coaches. Thus, the most essential element of these four elements is a strong educational program for coaches that ensures an educated, caring instructor or teacher. Teachers and coaches are powerful role models, and many times a child's self-esteem is very dependent on the teacher's approval or disapproval. Therefore, we feel strongly that college and university instructors need to direct a movement to improve their curricula in the instruction of social skills, so that the physical educators and coaches who are graduates of these programs are prepared to meet this challenge.

A child needs to learn that the way in which one competes is important and that treating teammates and opponents with respect will foster a better competitive atmosphere. Furthermore, kids should learn that treating each other with respect, following rules, and eliminating negative pressure will increase the team's enjoyment. Fun will become synonymous with team competition.

How do we attain these goals? Merely putting children into competitive situations is not enough. We need to ensure social and emotional growth. Can we teach children to become good teammates and foster positive self-esteem? We can if we follow the linking steps in this chapter plus choose sound philosophical sports programs for our children.

So then, how do we forge a link between competition and cooperation in the physical education curriculum? We will present a big-picture outlook as we look at a continuum of the preschool years through the high school program.

THE PRIMARY YEARS: PRESCHOOL THROUGH GRADE 3

In their early childhood years, children are not ready for a competitive physical education curriculum. Young children learn motor skills best through a play-oriented approach. Beginning movers move mostly out of curiosity and imagination. Children move to explore, to take risks, and to have fun. Play, and the resulting movements, is basic to the motor development of young children.

The knowledgeable physical education teacher realizes that a three- to six-year-old child's desire to move and explore is very strong. It is our job to create a play environment that encourages children to take risks by climbing, crawling under objects, balancing on objects, jumping from and jumping over objects, and hanging from and maneuvering through and around objects.

If provided with a creative play environment, young children can move and explore at their own rate of confidence in their abilities. Children who have an opportunity to take risks and succeed will become more confident movers as they grow and mature. However, a creative play environment isn't the only aspect of a young child's movement curriculum.

A second aspect of a movement curriculum is a movement education or exploration method for introducing motor skills to young children during physical education class. Using this approach, the children are encouraged to explore movement with or without equipment through a series of questions asked by the teacher that encourage the children to answer with creative movement. Using this method, children do not compare or naturally compete for the best movement sequence but rather perform at their own rate of exploration. Very little comparison of one another's skill level occurs during this method of delivering physical education. All children can experience success and have fun using movement education and hopefully develop a sense of competency. Competent and confident movers will result from this approach.

Fortunately, there are a number of resources available, such as Terry Orlick's book, *The Second Cooperative Sports and Games Book,* Marianne Torbert's *Follow Me: A Handbook of Movement Activities for Children,* and Steve Grineski's *Cooperative Learning in Physical Education,* which have specific cooperative learning activities for physical education classes. Activities found in our books, *Team Building Through Physical Challenges* and *More Team Building Challenges,* can also be adapted for young children.

Additionally, other ideas and activities that could be used by teachers and physical educators include the following:

1. Divide the children into small groups, give them interesting pieces of equipment (such as balls, hoops, wands, scoops, jump ropes, etc.), and have them create a game or activity that requires cooperation.
2. Have the children perform partner stunts such as two or three person balances or safe pyramids.
3. Give small groups personal challenges with skill activities such as volleying a balloon, catching or throwing a ball.

In all cases, place emphasis on sharing equipment, helping friends pick up and put away equipment, and recognizing the pleasure of having a cooperative and helpful partner or partners.

A preschool and primary movement program should include the following components:

- Play centers that encourage gross motor movement and risk taking
- A movement education approach to skill learning
- Cooperative games and team building activities appropriate for young children
- Activities that encourage sharing and cooperation

THE INTERMEDIATE YEARS: GRADES 4 THROUGH 6

In chapter 3 we will discuss some ideas for introducing team building as a unit of activity in an intermediate, middle school, or secondary classroom. We like to start the school year for intermediate grades with team building activities because these activities give students a unique way to begin good habits of working together toward a common goal. This creates an atmosphere of camaraderie, of helping one another; students learn that failing is not terminal, but rather a bridge to success.

More and more competitive activities, lead-up games, relays, and team sports will be introduced in physical education during these years. We certainly feel the activities we are including in this book are very worthwhile and will be a positive step in this transition. We suggest integrating some of these activities into the classroom prior to teaching competitive sports in your class. These suggestions are consistent with the ones we will offer in chapter 3.

Students are very impressionable at this age. Their heroes are often students just a few years older. Perhaps you could invite varsity high school student athletes to come and discuss the importance of being a good teammate. Perhaps a parent who owns a business could discuss teamwork as it relates to his or her business. A band or orchestra teacher could show the tie-in to teamwork in the music field. In addition, display your state or district Code of Ethics for Athletes. Discuss the elements of the code and have the students write them down. A possible homework assignment would be to write an essay on the importance of one statement in the code of ethics.

Code of Ethics for Athletes (Minnesota)
1. Show respect for opponents at all times.
2. Accept the decisions of game officials.
3. Avoid offensive gestures or language.
4. Display modesty in victory and graciousness in defeat.
5. Show respect for public property and equipment.

Display the Code of Ethics for Spectators. Discuss the importance of this code of ethics. Perhaps you could do a role-playing exercise in the classroom showing poor spectator sportsmanship toward an official or player. You could have the students write a paragraph on one or each of the ethical behaviors listed below, and follow up with a debate on the issue of spectator expectations.

Code of Ethics for Spectators (Minnesota)
1. Take part in positive cheering and applaud good performances.
2. Work cooperatively with contest officials and supervisors in keeping order.
3. Refrain from making negative comments about officials, coaches, and participants.
4. Stay off the playing area at all times.
5. Show respect for public property and equipment.

Display the Code of Ethics for Coaches. During the intermediate years many children will be getting into competitive athletic programs in the community. Many community associations offer highly competitive traveling team programs in numerous sports or organized sports leagues such as youth basketball or baseball programs. We are concerned about the volunteer coaches of these programs, many of whom participated in such programs as children. As physical educators, we see a distinct separation of our curriculum area from that of highly competitive community programs. However, many people see sport or athletic programs as the twin of physical education. Innumerable people who have suffered through bad physical education programs or insensitive coaches become either our lifelong enemies and detractors, or they carry on horrendous traditions of bad teaching or coaching.

If we are to make progress toward building strong teammates and making sportsmanship a priority then we must make certain our community sport programs use coaches who will instill these behaviors in their teams. The win-at-all-costs coaches need to be taught a new way of coaching kids. The techniques of building respect for self and others must be taught to these coaches before they begin coaching our kids. We advocate that this training be provided by community associations or groups such as the YMCA, AAU, or Junior Olympics. However, as physical educators, we need to begin teaching people these positive attitudes toward sports, teammates, and competitors long before the time a person decides to volunteer as a coach.

Code of Ethics for Coaches
1. Follow rules of the contest at all times.
2. Accept the decisions of contest officials.
3. Avoid offensive gestures or language.
4. Display modesty in victory and graciousness in defeat.
5. Avoid public criticism of game officials and participants.

Again, discuss this code of ethics. Display it in your classroom. Role play positive and negative coach behavior.

We see these codes of ethics as vital components of our role as physical educators. They also serve as an important tool in preparing students for good attitudes toward competitive activities. We can make a difference in fostering good sportsmanship, but we must make a commitment to teaching these behaviors and we must take the time to do it right.

Use the techniques in this chapter prior to competition to prepare students for progress toward building teams that are more fun in which to participate.

A good intermediate physical education and sports program should include the following components:

- An interdisciplinary approach; the classroom teacher and physical education teacher working together
- Teaching the code of ethics for players, spectators, and coaches
- Using high school role models to discuss the importance of responsible competitive behavior
- Identifying and rewarding proper social skills and good sportsmanship

THE SECONDARY YEARS: GRADES 7 THROUGH 12

During the high school years physical education teachers should have the pleasure of working as partners with educators in the school health programs. Educators should continue to reinforce the classroom concepts taught prior to these competitive years. One of the curriculum areas of secondary school health is the introduction of recognizing abusive or harassing behaviors. Students are also often asked to analyze the relationships among physical, social, and mental health. It seems to us that the secondary school health curriculum could incorporate the team building skills presented in chapter 3 and further relate those skills to topics of positive relationships, sportsmanship, respect, decision making, and other ways of dealing positively with teammates or classmates. We believe that an interdisciplinary relationship should exist between physical education and health.

In July of 1996, the Surgeon General reported that our high school students are less fit (and weigh more) than students were 30 years ago, and they need to become more active. Our physical education programs should respond to that information and place a high emphasis on physical fitness. Teaching youths to become fit for life by letting them design their own fitness programs should now be considered. For example, each student could evaluate a complete plan of diet and exercise in order to become a more physically fit adult.

Team building challenges provide an excellent way to begin the secondary school physical education experience. Physical education at this level should expose students to a wide variety of games and sports. Activities presented in class should be chosen because of their contribution to fitness and potential for lifelong participation. Team building concepts and activities should continue through middle school, with high school students designing their own challenges for their classmates.

Teaching students how to work on a team or how to coordinate one's efforts with others still needs to receive very high priority in physical education programs. Many activities that students will include in a fitness plan will still involve physical games. Cooperation will continue to lead to positive results.

Power of Choice

Allowing students to choose areas of interest can greatly enhance participation as students mature. The number of choices your program offers naturally depends on staff and facilities, but the concept of offering choices still is important.

Sample of Physical Activity Selection Chart
for Secondary Physical Education

September			
1. Fitness aerobics, walking, jogging	2. Golf	3. Tennis	4. Flag football
October			
1. Fitness aerobics, walking, jogging	2. Weight training	3. Soccer	4. Team building
November			
1. Weight training	2. Volleyball	3. Team building	4. Rollerblading
December			
1. Step aerobics	2. Badminton	3. Basketball	4. Dance
January			
1. Weight training	2. Team handball	3. Team building II	4. Dance II
February			
1. Weight training II	2. Badminton	3. Pickle ball	4. Volleyball

March			
1. Floor hockey	2. Fitness and weight training; aerobics, walking, jogging	3. Volleyball II	4. Team building

April			
1. Archery	2. Great games	3. Fitness	4. Softball

May			
1. Softball II	2. Great games II	3. Golf	4. Fitness

Every month, students could pick a new activity class from within the physical education curriculum. Make changes as they are needed. For example, if one class offering is exceptionally popular while another receives little interest, create two sections of the class that is better received and cancel the other one.

Remember, these are simply examples—offer classes that utilize your expertise and meet student needs. However, giving students the power to make choices offers them greater incentive to take ownership of their education. It is your responsibility to make good class offerings.

To continue building a healthy, respectful competitor, we must redouble our efforts through the secondary years. A good secondary program should include the following characteristics:

- Be closely tied with health
- Use the power of choice when designing curriculum
- Integrate team building rules and social skills into all competitive game situations (see chapter 4)

Chapter 3

FOLLOWING A SAMPLE PROGRAM

You can't do it alone. Be a team player, not an individualist, and respect your teammates. Anything you do you have to do as a team. Many records have been made, but only with the help of one's teammates.

Charlie Taylor
NFL wide receiver, as quoted in *The Edge*

The following sequential steps provide a blueprint for a series of lessons used with great success by a sixth grade classroom teacher in West St. Paul, Minnesota. The teacher, Leigh Anderson, introduced team building with a discussion and lecture followed by a team building unit. Mrs. Anderson recorded all lectures and activities in a journal. The following is an outline of these activities.

FIRST DAY: TEAMWORK DISCUSSION

Ask the students to identify companies listed among the Fortune 500. Talk about these companies, their products, and services. Discuss characteristics these companies look for in a prospective employee. Students often respond that these companies look for the following qualities:

1. Strong educational background
2. Reliability
3. Positive attitude
4. Experience
5. Neat appearance

Students are often surprised to discover that the number one skill many of these companies look for in employees is the ability to work as part of a team.

Ask if your students have been members of a team before? What kind of team? What are examples of teams that do not involve sports? Identify good experiences. Discuss negative experiences. Discuss what students think about team members who are quick to put down others who make mistakes; ask their opinions of the team members who complain, who don't get their way, or worse, who even cheat to win. Is being on a team with this type of person an unpleasant experience? Why?

Discuss how being encouraged by a teammate or praised by a team member makes you feel. Ask each student to evaluate his or her own behavior: What are examples of positive things you have done? What are some examples of negative behaviors you have witnessed. Have you ever done something that hurt a teammate's feelings?

Mrs. Anderson surveyed the other teachers in her building. The survey included the following: What is your least favorite thing concerning your teaching physical education? Ninety percent of the teachers responded that they did not like the way students treated one another. We want to change this behavior. As you conduct your lesson, give examples of put-downs and negative pressures. Explain that bad or hurtful words, frowns, and impatient attitudes are not going to help your team accomplish anything positive. Give examples of encouraging words and how the effect of these words creates a different attitude or environment.

SECOND DAY: TEAM BUILDING LEAD-UP

Begin this lesson with a review. Discuss and identify with the students what teamwork encompasses and why teamwork is important. Then ask the students to respond, in writing, to the following:

1. Relate a pleasant team experience.
2. Relate an unpleasant team experience.
3. Relate a time when you created a pleasant experience for your team or teammate.
4. Relate a time when you created an unpleasant experience for a team or teammate.

Mrs. Anderson states that the responses to these requests provided her class with a great amount of discussion material. Many students volunteered answers or experiences. They had definite ideas about the positive characteristics they wanted in their teammates.

THIRD DAY: INTRODUCTORY TEAM BUILDING ACTIVITY

Discuss the three roles that will be assigned to each team member or team while students are participating in team building activities: organizer, encourager, and praiser. The challenges used for examples can be found in two books published by Human Kinetics, *Team Building Through Physical Challenges* and *More Team Building Challenges*.

Organizer. The organizer helps the team members understand the challenges by reading the organizer card and challenge card to the team.

Put a challenge card on an overhead projection or give a copy to each student. Go through the challenge card, step by step, just as an organizer would in a group. Do the same activity using an organizer card. Point out that an organizer cannot call the teacher over to discuss the information until all the group members can answer all the questions on the organizer card.

Encourager. An encourager must use positive encouragement while a teammate is attempting a challenge.

Discuss why an encourager is needed. The encourager should encourage the whole team as well as individual effort or performance. Use a predetermined list of encouraging phrases (see figure 3.1). Brainstorm a list of phrases the students can use. Make copies of this list for your groups.

ENCOURAGING PHRASES

Praise and encouragement are two ways we can all feel good about the team. Here are 9 ways to say "Very good!" Copy and laminate this list, or create your own.

1. Nice try. Good try.
2. You can do it.
3. Keep trying.
4. Way to go.
5. Practice and try again.
6. You're getting it.
7. Let's work together.
8. Wow, you almost got it.
9. Almost!!

Figure 3.1   Encouraging phrases.

Praiser. The praiser is assigned the task of praising specific acts or efforts.

Discuss the role of the praiser and why we need one. Review a list of praise phases (see figure 3.2). Once again brainstorm a list of positive adjectives or phrases your class can use.

Some students may wonder why you need both an encourager and a praiser. Mrs. Anderson asked her class why they thought the two roles were needed. Here are some of their responses:

1. "When things are not going well, it's good to hear encouraging words."
2. "It's nice to receive praise when things are going well."
3. "It gives more people a chance to say something nice."

Students may also ask why the roles of encourager and praiser must be assigned. One reason is that many people, children and adults, do not know how to offer praise or encouragement when working closely together. We want to put group members into situations where these actions must occur. By assigning these roles, students will begin to develop praise and encouragement as habits within the framework of the activities. These attributes are as important as any athletic skill.

Relate encouragement and praise to specific sports situations. If a student makes a basket during a physical education activity, does he or she thank the person from whom the pass was received? If a person plays defense well, but an opponent scores anyway, do we encourage that person by saying "Good effort."? We need to model praise and encouragement, find ways to demonstrate our actions, reinforce the words and phrases, and continue to expect our students to praise and encourage.

PRAISE PHRASES

Praise and encouragement are two ways we can all feel good about the team. Here are 25 ways to say "Very good!" Copy and laminate this list, or create your own.

1. Good for you!
2. You did that very well.
3. Couldn't have done it better myself.
4. You're doing fine.
5. Now you've figured it out.
6. Outstanding!
7. Good work.
8. You figured that out fast.
9. You did well today.
10. Nice going.
11. You're getting better every day.
12. You're learning fast.
13. You make it look easy.
14. You did a lot of work today!
15. Keep it up!
16. Nice job.
17. That's really nice.
18. That's great.
19. Way to go!
20. That's the way to do it.
21. Good thinking.
22. Keep up the good work.
23. That's the right way to do it.
24. You remembered!
25. I've never seen anyone do it better.

Figure 3.2   Praise phrases.

FOURTH DAY: INTRODUCTORY PHYSICAL CHALLENGES

Mrs. Anderson's class began doing some introductory physical challenges on the fourth day of their teamwork adventure (examples: Tire Bridge, The Great Communicator, The Whole World). Tire Bridge and The Whole World are described in *Team building through physical challenge*. The Great Communicator is described in the appendix of this book. However, there are two intermediate steps you can add to this sequence.

Trust Falls

A trust fall occurs when one group member falls backward and is caught in the arms of his or her teammates. The falling team member must rely on the integrity of the group. This activity must be done on a crash pad or tumbling mat, and it requires a commitment from the group members to be responsible for the safety of one another.

The students falling backward should put their arms at their sides or cross their arms in front of their chests. The student should fall with his or her body stiff and straight. The group members catching their teammate should interlock arms and provide support for the falling member (see figure 3.3).

Figure 3.3   Trust falls.

The Great Communicator

This activity provides group members the opportunity to speak and listen to one another (see the appendix for complete instructions). Allow as many students to be the Great Communicator as possible. You may need to set a time limit (such as five minutes) to allow each student a turn to lead the group. You may also need to extend the activity into the next day's lesson.

USING PRAISE AND ENCOURAGEMENT

Another way of teaching the skills of praise and encouragement was given to us by Debbie Vigil, a 1994 NASPE elementary physical education Teacher of the Year. Ms. Vigil demonstrated her technique at a conference on facilitating responsibility through physical activity. She reinforces our belief that you cannot just tell students to praise and encourage one another, but you must teach them what praise and encouragement actually is and give them the time to practice these skills. We offer here her brief, introductory lesson on praise and encouragement.

With your large group or class, pose this question, "What is praise and when would you use it?" Provide a large chart with the heading, "Praise," in large letters. Beneath the heading write two subheadings, "Hear" and "See" (see figure 3.4).

PRAISE	
See	**Hear**

ENCOURAGEMENT	
See	**Hear**

Figure 3.4   The see-and-hear chart.

Ask the students to give examples of praise you can hear. List these under the "Hear" column. Follow this by asking students to give examples of praise you can see. Again, list their responses on the chart under the "See" column.

Duplicate this process by using an encouragement chart. When your students finish giving examples of encouragement that they can hear or see, and you are convinced they understand the difference between praise and encouragement, give them an opportunity to practice using these terms in a physical activity such as the following one we describe.

Put the students into groups of six. Each group will practice the rope-jumping skill called the Egg Beater (see figure 3.5). As four students turn the ropes, one student will be the jumper. The sixth student will be the recorder for the group. The turners and jumper positions should rotate so that all the turners get to jump. You can add the advanced skill of jumping a short rope inside the egg beater as well.

While the jumpers practice their jumping skills, the turners should practice their praise and encouragement skills. The recorder will record the responses of the jumping team on a social skills observation sheet (see figure 3.6). Provide a worksheet, pencil, and clipboard for the recorder. The task of recorder does not have to rotate.

Figure 3.5   The Egg Beater.

SOCIAL SKILLS OBSERVATION SHEET		
Name	See	Hear

Figure 3.6   The social skills observation sheet.

After the students have had time to practice the physical skill of rope jumping and the social skills of praising and giving encouragement, bring them back into a large group for discussion. The recorders can now give the class their information on their observations.

Reporting to the large group not only gives the students recognition for their social skills, but it also allows the class to evaluate what has occurred during the activity. Additionally, you may pose some questions to the class at this time:

- Were any put-downs or criticisms used?
- How do put-downs make you feel?
- How did being praised make you feel?
- How were you encouraged?
- Is it hard to praise another person?
- Was it hard to receive the praise or encouragement?

Ms. Vigil's lesson is simply one way to use praise and encouragement in an activity lesson. These social skills need to be practiced and reinforced just as we practice and reinforce physical skills. This lesson can be modified to any grade level. You may also wish to try the game Rip Flag Scramble, which is described in chapter 5, using the polite rules.

TEAM BUILDING TIPS

After following these outlined steps preparing your class for team building, you are ready to introduce some of the problem-solving activities presented in the team building books. Start with some of the introductory challenges and move on to some of the intermediate challenges. Do not move too quickly into the advanced challenges. When you first start doing the challenges you may observe some of the following behaviors:

- Some individuals begin a challenge too quickly, without discussing strategies or informing teammates of their intentions.
- Teams do not look at the challenge in its entirety. They will be so anxious to begin that their preliminary movements may have a negative effect on the next step in solving the challenge.
- Teams may not discover the strengths and weaknesses of their group. Often times the most dominant student will want to go first, but that student may not be the correct choice to be the first person to begin.
- Groups may make the same mistake over and over. They might not discuss why a mistake is occurring, or they may abandon a solution too soon without discovering ways to improve upon their attempt.
- Groups may continue with an incorrect solution too long without seeing the need to try something different.

- Teams may abandon a solution too quickly because it did not work the first time.
- Teams may overlook a good idea simply because it came from someone who does not have a great deal of credibility with the group.

Teachers and coaches, remember, be role models, encourage, and praise your class. Do not be too quick to help with solutions, allow the students to struggle before offering help. As teammates work together for a few class periods, they begin to see the value of helping and encouraging one another and to appreciate the achievements of the entire group.

EVALUATING YOUR PROGRAM

After two or three class periods of team building, have the students evaluate the experience. Use a team report card (see appendix) or do what Mrs. Anderson's class did. Her students were assigned the task of writing an evaluation of how well their team worked together. They included what they did right as well as what went wrong. Some of their comments follow:

- We didn't get upset when we made mistakes.
- Our team was successful because we shared ideas.
- No one gave put-downs, only put-ups.
- We worked very well together. I was proud of my team.
- We got frustrated, but we encouraged and praised well.
- Everybody said good things about each other, we encouraged each other and that made me feel good.
- We talked each other through the tough things. We cheered each other on and didn't use put-downs.
- We cooperated and listened to each other. The challenges were difficult, but we got by them working together.
- Our group talked over ideas before trying the challenge. I think that is why we were successful.

Although it is not necessary to do a team building unit before using activities from this book, we think you will find that preparing the students with the physical challenges of team building will enhance the positive attitudes they can develop from the activities presented here. Linking the physical challenges to the upcoming physical activities will make the next step, achieving good attitudes in traditional sports and games, successful as well.

Competitive activities can bring out the best in children when led by an informed, respectful, and committed adult, but anything can be harmful if it is directed by an unknowing person. When led by an informed, respectful, and committed adult, a child can be motivated to excel in competitive sports. Cooperation and respect can be infused into all competitive sports and games. This may have to start in your home, your classroom, or your school. If each one of us commits wholeheartedly to changing attitudes toward competition in our gyms, we will make a difference in the lives of countless children.

We can work toward developing successful, cooperative competitors at any age level by using the following outline:

- Lecture and discussion
- Team building questions and discussion
- The roles students will take in the physical challenges
- Trust falls
- The Great Communicator
- Introductory, intermediate, and advanced team building activities
- Activities in this book
- Evaluation and discussion
- Traditional sports and games

Chapter 4

GETTING STARTED

Photo by Dan Midura

The purpose of life is to be a growing, contributing human being.

David McNally
Even Eagles Need a Push

L inking team building and cooperative activities to competition isn't about finding new magical activities. We advocate changing competitive behaviors and attitudes. If you can make competition more fun, exciting, and healthy for the participants because of their attitude changes, it will not be solely because of the activities you use.

Please do not think that we feel team building activities are the only activities that produce the desired behaviors. They comprise just a small percentage of our curriculum. However, the attitudes we desire our students to exhibit are fostered in a very healthy way through the team building challenges.

REINFORCING HEALTHY ATTITUDES

What, then, do we do with other games and activities to reinforce and teach good attitudes or respect? First of all, let us suggest that we need to transfer the responsibility for good behavior from the teacher to the student. Instead of creating endless lists of rules to which students must adhere, we need to develop reasonable and rational expectations for our students to follow, that is, a set of rules based on student responsibility for acceptable behavior.

Consider this simple example from our running activities. First, we have three expectations for safe traveling in the gym: no falling (this includes sliding on the floor), no touching other people (unless asked to tag others), and no voices (which eliminates yelling, animal or car noises, and other extraneous noises). We expect students to move responsibly so that their own safety and the safety of others is given the highest priority.

Second, we have an expectation of honesty in running games: if a chaser says that he or she has tagged a student, the student is considered caught (or must follow whatever the consequence happens to be). This simple expectation eliminates the endless time that is wasted arguing or debating whether someone has been tagged or not ("No you didn't." "I didn't feel it." "You only touched my hair."). If the chaser says you are caught, you are caught. Of course the chasers have to make a commitment to be honest. Classmates have to develop a trust in each other so that the statement of the chaser is not impugned. As the teacher, you may have to, on occasion, deal with situations where someone is not correctly following these expectations. But we deal with minor irritations every day of our lives. So be prepared to act quickly when someone behaves in a way not consistent with the expectations for the game. If the expectations are clear and reasonable, the students will accept them. Above all, be consistent, hold fast to the need for the expectations.

By having clear and reasonable expectations, you create a climate where participation becomes the focal point of the activity. The objective of winning the activity can be replaced by the enjoyment of the activity.

In one of the running games, Rip Flag Scramble, we use our polite rules. As students run from base to base (free places where they cannot be caught), they must say something polite to the student standing on the base they wish to occupy. "Excuse me, please." "Pardon me." "Thank you for your base." "Happy Tuesday, good-bye." "How kind of you to give me your base." These are all phrases that begin to permeate the gym. Students cannot help but laugh and smile at all the polite things being said around them. As the teacher, you will find it difficult not to smile and laugh when you hear your students in constant polite speech. Students simply are not to use words that are not polite. All that politeness changes the atmosphere in your gym. It is very hard to get upset with your classmates when they are speaking kindly and politely.

As we said earlier, if you want to see certain behaviors develop, you must model the behavior, demonstrate the behavior, reinforce the behavior, and give practice time for the behavior. If politeness is a behavior you wish to see in your class, do you expect the students to say "thank you" each time you hand them equipment? Do you respond by saying "you're welcome" even if it means repeating the phrase 29 times in a row? Good, positive behaviors rarely happen by chance, but they can be taught and developed.

EXPLAINING YOUR EXPECTATIONS

When we created rules or expectations for team building activities, we did so to develop a better environment, better attitudes toward class-mates, and better attitudes toward achieving a defined goal. When dealing with competitive activities, you should expect certain behaviors from your students, which help to build better relationships between individuals whether they are teammates or opponents. As with team building activities, there are some standard operating procedures that should be followed from kindergarten through high school. These procedures are not rules, but expectations of what should take place in class. Following are some examples of the behavior we expect from our students:

1. Before play begins, the teams shake hands with their opponents and wish them good luck.
2. Each day rotate the task of being the team captain or leader. The captains are responsible for making decisions and judgments and solving disagreements as well as assigning positions of players.
3. Teams must verbally use praise and encouragement.

4. Students are not to call one another by last names, nor are they to use put-downs during play. Since decisions on disagreements are left to the captains, student players should not complain.
5. Teams shake hands after games and congratulate opponents as well as teammates.

You must be consistent in creating expectations that reflect respect of others. Talk about your expectations often, reinforce that behavior. Change will occur. Acknowledge and reward demonstrations of sportsmanship and team skills as much or more than skill performance. We *can* make a link between cooperation and competition.

Before we leave this chapter and move on, we would like to answer one question that we have heard often regarding expectation number four in the list of expected player behavior. "Why do you eliminate the use of calling students by last names in class?" If you have used our team building activities, you may have observed that this is the one consistent rule we have in every single problem-solving challenge.

We believe that the use of first names helps to create a warm attitude, fosters a more intimate feeling of respect among teammates, and reduces the negative connotation that the use of last names can carry. To hear someone say "Nicole, nice set," sounds kinder and more pleasant than "Hey Cook, good play." To hear "Josh, reach out your hand," sounds softer than "Anderson, help me." Using first names tends to break down the barriers that keep students from caring about one another. Addressing people by their last names only, allows you to keep others away, and inhibits you from developing the closeness that permits friends to hold one another accountable for their actions and reactions. The values of respect and responsibility, which are so vital to good competition, require a courtesy and consideration among teammates and opponents. We feel that requiring students to call each other by their first names makes this process more enjoyable and easier to implement.

USING THE ACTIVITIES IN THIS BOOK

The activities that follow in chapter 5 do not need the support of team building challenges. They stand on their own merits. They can be taught without tying them to the team building challenges, yet they offer a nice balance and follow-up to the attitudes developed through team building. They offer a link between team building and competitive activities.

We have chosen 30 activities to be included in this book. The first six activities in chapter 5 are designed to take five to 10 minutes to administer or complete. The next 12 activities are expected to take 15 to 30 minutes of your class time. The final 12 activities will require an entire class period or longer.

The activities presented in chapter 5 are activities that we have found to work with our students, activities that motivate them. Many are activities that can be used with different lessons or themes throughout the course of a school year. We do not view these activities as a magical cure for anything, but they provide ways for students to enjoy themselves while playing and practicing concepts or skills, and they help students build positive attitudes toward each other and competition.

One final note: these activities are presented for anyone who wishes to teach physical activities to children, not just for physical education specialists. Some of the games and activities need to be taught first in their most simplistic form so that students clearly understand the procedure of the activities. Once the activity is learned, you can add variations in order to increase participation, decrease waiting time, and limit any elimination features from the activity. Such variations usually are noted in each of the games and activities found in the book.

Part II
Games and Activities

Chapter 5

COMPETITIVE AND COOPERATIVE ACTIVITIES

A positive attitude requires courage because it is a decision not to be defeated no matter what challenges life presents.

David McNally
Even Eagles Need a Push

LAST RUNNER OUT

Lesson Objectives

The purpose of Last Runner Out is to provide a training or warm-up activity that focuses students on controlling their running pace in addition to teaching them to work together as a group.

Grade Range

This activity can be taught to any grade level.

Activity Area

Last Runner Out can be conducted indoors or outdoors. Even though the size of the running oval is not crucial to the activity, we recommend an oval approximately 50 meters in perimeter but not smaller than this size. If you build your oval within the boundaries of a basketball court, be sure to leave enough passing room between the out-of-bounds line of the court and any wall space that may be near the court.

Equipment Needed

The only equipment necessary may be cones to build a running oval.

Activity Description

If your group numbers more than about fifteen, put the students into two equal-sized groups (see figure 5.1). Group 1 lines up single file at

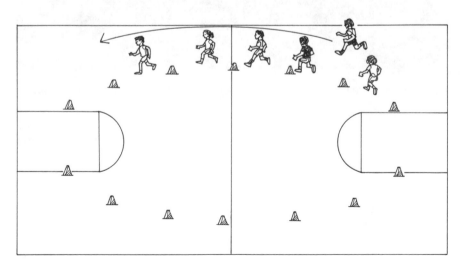

Figure 5.1   Last Runner Out.

a designated starting point on the track. The first person begins jogging a slow to moderate pace with the entire group following in single file. On your signal, such as a hand clap, the last runner sprints around the outside of the group to the front of the line and becomes the new jog leader. On each succeeding signal the last runner takes a turn sprinting to the front and then slows to the jogging pace. The group continues around the track until the first runner becomes the leader once again. At this point, the runners may walk once or partway around the track. Group 2 then takes the track and starts their activity.

Competitive and Cooperative Features

Even though this activity is designed primarily to be cooperative in nature, students can feel a sense of competitiveness by seeing how fast each one can get to the front of the line when it is his or her turn to sprint or run fast. Additionally, if you give the students a running time limit, such as three minutes, a group can be motivated competitively to see how many laps their group can achieve during the time limit.

A group showing good cooperative skills will keep their running line together. Students will remain close to the person ahead without spreading out the jogging line. They will communicate if the jogging pace is too slow, too fast, or perfect.

Safety Tips

If students turn to look at runners behind them, they risk tripping or stepping on a cone.

Special Behaviors to Observe

1. Runners often jog too fast.
2. Encourage joggers on line to stay close to the person in front.

Teaching Tips

1. Remind the last runner out to slow down upon reaching the front of the line in order to keep the jogging line together (slow to the existing pace).
2. Once you have taught this activity to your class, you can have the nonjogging group concentrating on another activity such as stretching, a skill practice activity, rope jumping, and so forth.

Adaptations

1. If you have students who have difficulty with endurance, have them begin at the end of the line so they become the first persons to sprint. The teacher can always control the pace, keep it slow if needed.

2.   You can do this activity outdoors with any size group traveling any reasonable distance. If the group is very large, as the last runner reaches the front of the line (or designated place, such as the halfway mark of the group), that runner could call "Last runner out." If the groups are small, the last runner could see when the person makes it to the front.

3.   Groups can continue the activity for a designated distance or time.

4.   If you have a runner who cannot sprint up to the front of the line, that runner could simply turn back and let the group jog around the minitrack and catch up to the runner, who simply enters the line in his or her order.

Special Comments

This is a favorite activity of ours. We find it to be an excellent, focused, controlled running activity. Generally, all students can participate well in Last Runner Out.

FIRST RUNNER TO THE BACK

Lesson Objectives

This jogging activity is to be used as a warm-up activity. It is designed to reinforce the concept of pacing, introduce baton passing, and provide a controlled running warm-up. In addition, it requires the group to work together for the best results. This lesson should be taught after Last Runner Out.

Grade Range

First Runner to the Back is suitable for fourth grade and above.

Activity Area

This activity can be done indoors or outdoors. An area the size of a basketball court is sufficient. You will need to set up an oval track, using cones, approximately 50 meters in perimeter.

Equipment Needed

Approximately 16 cones are needed to make the track. Have 4–6 track batons available.

Activity Description

If your class is larger than 16 students, divide the class into two equal groups. One group will run at a time (see figure 5.2). The first running group begins by forming a single file line on the track. Give a track baton to every third or fourth runner, starting at the back of the group. As the students begin jogging forward, they begin passing the batons to the front of the group. When the jog leader receives a baton, he or she sprints around the track and catches up to the last jogger in line. The person who sprinted passes the baton forward upon joining the jogging line. As each student becomes the jog leader, that student will jog at a very easy pace until he or she receives a baton. Upon receiving the baton, each jog leader then sprints around the track and catches up to the last person in line. The group continues jogging until the first jog leader works his or her way back to the position of jog leader. Upon receiving the baton a second time, the leader is instructed to walk.

The jogging group needs to jog at a slow to moderate pace. Each person needs to stay close to the person in front. If the jogging group spreads out, this activity begins to unravel. They must stick together as a group.

It is very helpful to demonstrate the baton pass before the students begin jogging. We recommend that the students reach back with the right hand. The arm should be extended backward so that it is almost parallel to the ground (simply place your thumb at your side, palm facing back, and extend your arm back and up). The baton should be placed on the hand with a downward motion. After receiving the baton in the right hand, the student switches the baton to the left hand and passes it forward. We suggest that the students say the name of the runner directly in front as a signal for that student to reach back. We do not want the students turning to look back.

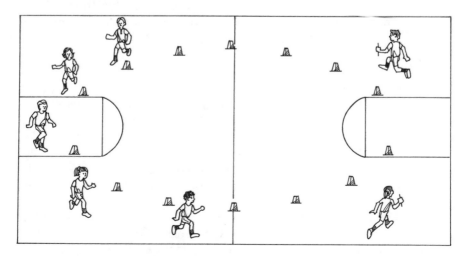

Figure 5.2   First Runner to the Back.

Competitive and Cooperative Features

This activity is primarily a cooperative effort. The group members need to set a running pace that allows the entire group to run at a comfortable speed and at a pace that allows the main group to keep together. Additionally, the activity requires group members to pass the baton in a manner that assists their teammates. The better the passing, the more personal success each runner will receive. The better the passing, the more efficient the activity becomes. The better the passing, the more enjoyable the activity will be.

If there is a competitive feature to this activity, it might be found in the speed a runner runs when it is his or her turn to be a sprinter. A group may take a competitive pride in how efficiently their group performs; for example, they do not drop the baton at all, they can all complete their passes without looking behind them, they can complete all their passes and sprinting within a specified time limit.

If you want to make this activity more competitive, the group could be challenged to see how many sprinters could be sent out and catch up to the back of the group within a certain time limit. They could be challenged to see if they could complete the activity while being timed with a stopwatch.

We recommend that you teach the activity as a cooperative venture first so that the group knows the expected running pattern very well.

Safety Tips

1. If students turn to look back at the runners behind, they risk tripping or stepping on a cone.
2. It has been our observation that students are more likely to turn toward the person behind if they reach back with the left hand when jogging counterclockwise. We recommend reaching back with the right hand.

Adaptations

1. Once you have taught this activity to your group of students, you can have the students who are not running work on another assignment such as a designated group of exercises or specific activities.
2. If you have a student who cannot sprint around the track and catch up to the group, that person could simply step inside the track, let the group pass, and reenter the jogging line at the rear of the group.
3. This activity could be done by small groups jogging a specific distance or for a specific time. Once the leader receives the baton, that person could simply peel back to the end of the jogging line and begin passing the baton forward.

Special Comments

1. Runners often jog too fast.
2. Do not allow students to slap the baton into another person's hand.
3. Remind the jog leaders not to sprint until they have the baton. Often a jog leader will take off chasing the person at the end of the line without having a baton.

RIP FLAG SCRAMBLE

Lesson Objectives

This running game incorporates the basic locomotor skill of running as well as the skills of dodging, changing directions, and grasping. This game provides the participants with a great deal of activity in which students can play with one another rather than just against one another. It should be used as a vehicle to teach the awareness of others while running safely. Most importantly, it can be used as a game that reinforces friendly attitudes and polite behaviors.

Grade Range

This activity is suitable for any grade level.

Activity Area

A basketball court-sized area provides plenty of space for a class of up to 35 students. This activity can be done indoors as well as outdoors.

Equipment Needed

Each student will need one rip flag and one rip flag belt. In addition, you will also need five or six bases, preferably flat, indoor, nonsliding-type bases.

Activity Description

Rip Flag Scramble is a simple, yet very effective, running game that allows for a great deal of participation. To prepare for the game, randomly place five or six bases throughout the play area (see figure 5.3). Give each student one rip flag belt and one rip flag. To choose chasers, take the flags from about six students. Use any organizational technique to choose the chasers such as "Everyone with an August birthday, please give me your flag."

Explain that a student will be a chaser only until he or she rips off someone's flag. When a chaser successfully grasps a flag, the chaser puts

Figure 5.3   Rip Flag Scramble.

that flag on his or her own belt and becomes a runner. The person losing the flag temporarily becomes the new chaser. A person is only a chaser when he or she does not have a flag. If a flag falls onto the floor, anyone without a flag may pick it up and put it onto his or her belt.

The bases are to be used as safe or free places. A student standing on a base is safe from the chasers. However, if another student comes to an occupied base, the student on the base must leave. The last student to come to a base becomes the temporary owner of that base. A student must go to a different base before returning to any base on which the student was previously standing.

One of the most important elements of this game is what we call our polite rules. Students arriving at an occupied base must speak politely to the student on that base. We use phrases such as the following: "Pardon me." "Excuse me, please." "Thank you for your base." "Happy day, see you soon." Students may not push someone off a base and say "Get out of here." Also, do not allow screaming, yelling, or loud voices, which all lead to self-control problems.

By using the polite rules, an attitude of friendly play is developed without the feeling of competing against one another.

Competitive and Cooperative Features

This game is designed to be cooperative in nature and to teach students to enjoy participating with everyone in the entire class. However, competitively, students will try to keep from getting caught, chasers will try to succeed in stealing a flag, and students will enjoy removing a classmate from a base.

Cooperatively, students will need to respond properly to the polite requests received during the game. Since there are no clear winners or losers in this game, the class should find this game not only a lot of fun, but one that creates no anxiety or nervousness.

As students get to know the abilities of one another throughout the course of the time they spend together, there may be those students who are secure enough in themselves to allow some lower-ability chasers to catch their flags, thereby not only allowing those less able students a chance to try to run, stand on the free bases, and keep their flags again, but giving the secure persons the fun of chasing others as well.

Safety Tips

1. Refer to the polite rules. Reinforce these situations.
2. Students should have had an introduction to safe travel in your teaching or game area.
3. Flags should be worn hanging from the hip.

Special Behaviors to Observe

1. Occasionally you will find some students standing on the perimeter of the play area, not running. Keep them moving.
2. Sometimes a chaser will rip many flags from runners and forget to put one onto his or her belt.
3. Stop any behavior not consistent with the polite rules. Insist that students use the polite phrases.

Teaching Tips

Refer once again to the organization suggestion for choosing chasers. Each of our students has an assigned personal space in our gymnasium, so we use those as the starting places for the game. Generally, this game is played for 4–8 minutes. If you choose to play for a longer period of time, we suggest providing short rest periods.

Adaptations

This game is so simple to conduct that we have not found it necessary to make any special adaptations other than to provide a way for any student who simply cannot get a flag to do so.

Special Comments

To observe students running about using polite phrases can be quite humorous. When students are polite, it becomes impossible to get upset with one another. Flags change ownership so often that students do not have time to worry about who is a chaser or who owns a base.

FASTEST TAG IN THE WORLD

Lesson Objectives

The purpose of this activity is to provide a vigorous and exciting warm-up game. Running, dodging, changing directions, stopping, and safe tagging are to be reinforced.

Grade Range

This game can be played at any grade level.

Activity Area

This game can be played in an area the size of a basketball court. After teaching the game and playing it a few times, you may wish to reduce the area slightly in order to make it even more challenging. Do, however, have four distinct boundary lines. Fastest Tag in the World can be played indoors or outdoors.

Equipment Needed

No equipment is needed for this game unless you need cones for marking boundary lines (see the adaptations section for an exception).

Activity Description

Students begin by standing in their personal spaces. Be certain no one can touch another person or wall space. All students are chasers and all students can be tagged by every other student. When you clap your hands, all students attempt to run from each other while trying to tag other people. Once a person is tagged, he or she is temporarily frozen. While frozen, a student may not move his or her feet and legs or bend at the hips. A frozen student may however, reach out and tag anyone running. If two students tag one another at the same time, they are both frozen (see figure 5.4).

After about 15 seconds, in which time most of the students have been frozen, clap your hands and say "Fastest tag in the world; you're free" (or give a signal of your choice). Everyone is unfrozen and is free to run and tag again. You will probably clap your hands and allow freedom to the students 6–10 times before calling for a break.

This game is intended to be a quick warm-up or introductory activity in class. It should only be played for a few minutes. There is no need to declare winners in this game.

Competitive and Cooperative Features

Tagging as many other people as possible or keeping from getting tagged by others will create a competitive nature to the game.

Figure 5.4 Fastest Tag in the World.

The cooperative features of this game may require some reinforcing on your part. Students need to be taught that everyone will get caught from time to time, if not frequently. There might be times when they will get caught immediately when the teacher calls out, "Fastest tag in the world; you're free." A student may be standing right behind another person and tag the person as soon as the call is made.

Students might need to be encouraged to let the person closest to them go free, or they may need to be encouraged not to tag the same person first each time the game continues. This game usually invokes a lot of laughter and fun due to the quick responses in the game. Point out that the most fun occurs when kids realize they are all playing with each other even though they might be playing against one another. Individual winners are not easily identified (nor is it necessary to identify individual winners), as this activity is intended to be a warm-up or introductory game.

Safety Tips

1. Be sure to have well-defined boundary lines. If someone runs out of bounds, he or she is temporarily frozen until your next signal to run.

2. Do not play this game if you have not taught your students expectations for safe running and tagging.
3. Remind students that people will be running in all directions and to be aware of all others around them.

Teaching Tips

1. Do not allow loud voices or yelling. Students need to hear your signal for running as well as your voice.
2. Do not allow hard tagging. Remember: a tag is a touch.

Adaptations

One adaptation is to have a designated student run throughout the activity area tagging frozen students. Students are freed when tagged by this person. You may wish to have this person wear a colored jersey or carry an object such as a foam Frisbee so the person is visible to everyone else. Do something to make this person stand out.

Another adaptation is to periodically move the boundary lines closer together in order to make the running area smaller.

Special Comments

Please rename this game Fastest Tag in _____ (your school, community, state, etc.).

EDW 500

Lesson Objectives

EDW 500 is a warm-up or training activity that combines running with a variety of exercises or specifically designated training activities. Students will work with a partner during this time.

Grade Range

This activity can be conducted at any grade level.

Activity Area

This activity can be conducted indoors or outdoors. We suggest making a running track or oval just inside the boundary lines of a basketball court. The oval should be approximately 50 meters in perimeter.

Equipment Needed

Approximately 16 cones will be used to make the track (about one cone per two students). Additional equipment will be determined by the exercises or activities you wish to incorporate. As an example, if you wish to include rope jumping as an activity in this lesson, you will need one rope per two students. In almost every case, you will need one piece of equipment for each set of partners to share. Additionally, you may want to make 2–4 posters to list exercises or activities for the participating students to read.

Activity Description

One student from each set of partners will begin by standing next to a cone on the running track (see figure 5.5). This student will be the first running partner. The other student from each set will begin by standing near the same cone, inside the track. This student will be the first exercising partner. On the teacher's signal, the first running partner begins running one lap around the track. At the same time, the exercising partner begins the first exercise or activity designated by the teacher or the exercise chart.

As the running partner completes the first lap around the track, the partners quickly trade assignments. Partner one exercises, partner two runs around the track. The partners continue alternating running and exercising

Figure 5.5   EDW 500.

until the five or six activities on the list are completed. The number of exercises or activities can vary according to your needs or desires.

Competitive and Cooperative Features

The competitive nature of this activity will tend to exhibit itself by the speed at which the students run as well as by the speed at which they perform their exercise challenges. You, as the teacher, may have to set some numerical goals for the students if you are not satisfied with the number of activity repetitions completed by the exercising partner. As an example, if a student is jumping rope while the running partner is running the track, you might be satisfied with any number of completed jumps that student accomplishes. However, you might want the jumper to set a goal to complete a minimum of 15 jumps before the running partner returns.

The cooperative features of this activity include keeping each other on task as to which is the next task to be completed, as well as running at a speed that allows the exercising partner to do his or her best without getting too tired. For example, if a running partner jogged very slowly while the exercising partner was doing a difficult activity such as push-ups, the exercising partner might get discouraged or dissatisfied with the runner. By running or jogging at a fast or reasonable speed, the running partner should be able to keep the exercising partner positively motivated.

Safety Tips

We suggest that each set of students begins next to a designated cone. If the students run counterclockwise, they should exit the track on the left hand side of their cone (as they face the cone while running toward it). They should exit the track before they pass the cone. The partner running onto the track should enter the track on the left hand side of the cone (as he or she faces the cone). In this manner, partners will avoid running into one another. If students on the track pass other runners, they should pass on the outside of the track (next to the other person's right shoulder) to avoid contact with other runners.

Special Behaviors to Observe

If the running partner jogs too slowly, the exercising partner will be working longer than other students. Students should run at a reasonable speed.

Teaching Tips

If you are not satisfied with the cooperation level of a group or feel that some students are deliberately avoiding the designated activities, you might require an exerciser to perform a minimum number of repetitions of an exercise before an exerciser becomes a runner. Students who run too fast often do not do their exercising properly.

Adaptations

Generally any adaptations will be due to a specific individual need. For example, if a student had an injured arm and could not do a push-up, the student could replace that exercise with either another exercise or a second set of a previous exercise.

Special Comments

Please rename this activity to reflect your school's name, or relate it to another activity. EDW refers to the initials of the school of one of the authors (D.M.).

RIP-OFF CHAMP

Lesson Objectives

This game will reinforce skills of running, dodging, and changing directions. Spatial awareness, agility, and body control should be demonstrated.

Grade Range

This game is suitable for grade 3 and above.

Activity Area

This game can be played on a basketball court-sized area. You will need four distinct boundary lines (see figure 5.6). This game can be played indoors or outdoors.

Equipment Needed

You will need one rip flag belt and two rip flags per student. You may also need cones for outdoor boundary markers.

Activity Description

Students begin by standing in their spaces with their rip flag belts and two flags. The flags should be hanging down from their hips (not front and back). On signal from the teacher (hand clap), the students begin chasing one another. Each will attempt to capture as many flags as possible. All captured flags are to be held in the hands. If a student loses one flag, he or she continues chasing the other students. If a player loses the second flag, he or she sits down immediately on the ground or floor with legs crossed.

Figure 5.6   Rip-Off Champ.

There are two ways to reenter the game. The first is for a sitting student to grasp the flag of a passing runner. The sitting student puts the flag on his or her belt and reenters the game. The second entry method depends on the number of captured flags the sitting student possesses. If a student has two or more flags, the student must put two flags on his or her belt and then reenter the game. If a student sees a flag on the floor, the student may pick it up and add it to his or her collection. Students may not take flags being held by their classmates.

Stop the activity after 60 to 90 seconds and have the students return to their spaces. Decide how to acknowledge multiple flag collectors. For example, you can acknowledge those students collecting five or more flags by having them stand and take a bow.

Have students who need flags raise their hands. Students with more than two flags can politely hand their extra flags to their needy friends. As soon as each student has two flags, repeat the game.

Competitive and Cooperative Features

The competitive nature of this game will be very apparent: students chasing one another attempting to steal many flags and collect them for themselves, students trying to gain entry back into the game if all their flags get taken from them.

The cooperative aspects of the game are not as apparent. One reason is that there are no teams, plus the fact that there are few, if any, opportunities to team up with another person. This is a game where the individual is really on his or her own.

For this game to work effectively, students must have respect for others as well as respect for the method of reentry into the game.

Students temporarily eliminated must sit on their seats with their legs crossed. With students sitting in this manner, the runners are afforded a much safer running environment. If students are allowed to lean over, lie down, or get up on their knees to grasp a flag from a runner, the runners may easily be tripped or tackled. We also use an honor system, which you can certainly change or adapt to meet the needs of your group. The main element of our honor system states that if sitting students have flags in their hands and they are instructed not to put those flags on their belts, then it is up to your group to honor that instruction. You simply cannot monitor this element perfectly. We feel that an honor system is essential.

Safety Tips

1. Students will be running in all directions. Be sure the students have received instruction on safe running procedures.
2. If a student runs out of bounds while being chased, he or she must give a flag to the chaser. If a student runs out of bounds and no one is in pursuit, no penalty is needed.
3. Do not allow loud voices or yelling.

Adaptations

One adaptation is to distribute flags of different colors. Chasers must collect their first (and possibly second) flag in a specific color. For example, you could require that the students must first get a red flag and then a yellow flag and then they may collect any flags in any order.

Another adaptation is to have one or two students carry a whole handful of extra flags (these students are not chasers). These students can rescue sitting students by handing them one or two flags. If either of these adaptations is used, you may wish to extend the length of each game from 60 to 90 seconds to a longer time frame.

Special Comments

As with any running game, safety is an important issue. It is essential that students have a commitment to safety. Students must not push or use their hands and arms to protect their flags or ward off classmates from taking flags. If you do not require this commitment to safe play, this game could turn into a very physical activity, which would negate the fun and value of this game.

COLOR TAG

Color Tag, and its variations, is one of the simplest and most basic tag games available, yet it continues to be a favorite of students. Color Tag can easily be played with any group of competitors or participants.

Lesson Objectives

The purpose of this game is to reinforce the skills of running, dodging, changing directions, and safe tagging.

Grade Range

This game can be played in any grade or age group.

Activity Area

This game can be played indoors or outdoors. You will need an open space such as a basketball court or a 30' × 60' area marked by cones. Students will cross the wide area, that is, run from side to side rather than end to end of the play area.

Equipment Needed

No equipment is needed for teaching this game, unless you need cones for marking boundaries.

Activity Description

Students begin by standing along one wide side of the play area (see figure 5.7). Three people will be designated chasers. The chasers begin by standing apart from one another near the middle of the play area.

The cues for running will be the colors that students are wearing on their clothing. If the teacher says "red," anyone wearing red will run to the

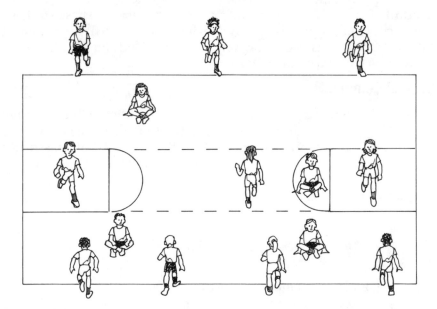

Figure 5.7   Color Tag.

opposite side of the play area. We recommend that only visible colors count toward the running cues. If a student is not wearing the called color, the student does not run. As soon as the runners cross the running space, the teacher calls another color. After the first call, students will most likely be running in opposite directions from some of their classmates.

If a chaser tags a runner, the runner sits down in that spot. Tagged runners sit on their seats with their legs crossed in front of them. If a sitting person tags a runner, the runner sits down and the tagger gets free entry back into the game.

There are a variety of ways you can begin a new game, for example, when all the runners get caught, when three runners are left, when a certain time limit expires, after a designated number of colors are called, and so forth. Choose a method for ending a game that is clear and defined for the students.

Have each of the chasers choose another student to take his or her place. Most often, we have students choose someone of the opposite gender as a replacement chaser. Most games take just a few minutes to complete so a number of students will have the opportunity to become chasers.

Competitive and Cooperative Features

This game offers both competitive and cooperative features. To remain in the game as long as possible without getting caught or to catch as many people as possible are obvious competitive features. Dodging, changing directions, and escaping can all be motivating to students who enjoy competition. Attempting to catch the fastest runners in class can also add to the competitive nature of the game.

Rescuing others, teaming up with another chaser to trap runners, and helping classmates find safe or clear running lanes can add to the qualities of cooperation. Allowing as many students as possible to have the opportunity to be a chaser adds to the enjoyment.

Safety Tips

1. Do not allow sliding.
2. Do not allow runners to jump over sitting students.
3. Keep your goal lines a safe distance away from any wall.
4. Remind students that a tag is a touch.
5. Remind students that after the first turn, runners will be running toward one another quite often, and they must be aware of other runners.

Teaching Tips

1. Runners should respond to a running cue within three seconds of the call.
2. Chasers should return to a designated area (such as half the distance between the goal lines) before each cue.

3. Students must commit themselves to accepting the fairness policy of believing a tagger who says he or she has tagged someone.
4. A lesson on safe running procedures should be taught before playing this game.

Adaptations

Two variations of this game are Letter Tag and Number Tag. In Letter Tag, students use the letters that appear in their proper first, middle, and last names as running cues. In Number Tag, students run when digits that appear in their telephone numbers (or home addresses) are called. If a student has more than one phone number in his or her family, have the student use the number most frequently used or the one that you would use to call them.

Once you have taught the basic format to this game, you can find additional ways to allow sitting students to reenter the game. One way of reentry would be if the sitting student tagged a passing chaser. Another way is for designated runners to carry a foam Frisbee and to tag sitting students with the foam Frisbee in order to rescue them. An additional way would be for a sitting student to raise a hand after sitting for three calls in a row. If a runner (or two runners) tags that person, the sitting person gets back into the game. We recommend that any student reentering the game be given free entry, that is, if a student stands up, he or she cannot be immediately tagged again.

Special Comments

1. It is common for students to wait after the teacher calls a running cue before they run. It is a strategy that often works in their favor. Other people get the attention of the chasers, which allows them safer passage across the running space. This strategy often slows down the game, however, and usually gives an advantage to the more skilled runners in class. We suggest that students run within three seconds of the teacher's call.
2. As mentioned before, students will be running in opposite directions of some of their classmates in this game. We strongly suggest that you teach a lesson on safe running expectations and procedures prior to playing this game.

ENCYCLOPEDIA TAG

Even though Encyclopedia Tag is a variation of Color Tag, we consider it separately because students can create their own sets of running cues. It becomes their own creative game, even though the format is basically the same as Color Tag.

Lesson Objectives

The purpose of this game is to reinforce the skills of running, dodging, changing directions, and safe tagging.

Grade Range

This game can be played in any grade or age group.

Activity Area

This game can be played indoors as well as outdoors. A basketball court-sized area would make an adequate playing area. Students will run across from side to side of the play area rather than from end to end.

Equipment Needed

No equipment is needed, unless you need marking cones for outdoor boundaries.

Activity Description

Students begin by standing on one side of the play area. Three designated chasers begin by standing apart from one another near the middle of the designated boundaries.

Students run from one side of the play area to the other side when running cues are called.

If a chaser tags a runner, the runner sits down near that spot. Tagged runners sit on their seats with their legs crossed in front of them. If a sitting person tags a runner, the runner sits down and the person tagging the runner gets free return entry into the game.

We use a variety of questions, statements, or experiences to determine the running cues for this game. The first time you play the game, we suggest that the teacher generate the running cues. The cues given should elicit a running response from a large group of students. Following are some example cues:

- Run if you have a pet.
- Run if you were born in Minnesota (name of your state).
- Run if you are wearing high-top tennis shoes.
- Run if you play a musical instrument (make this a grade-appropriate statement).
- Run if you have ever been in the principal's office (positive or negative).
- Run if you have ever attended a concert.

As you can see, the cues are endless. You can phrase statements to make sure nearly everyone runs at one time, or you can phrase statements so that smaller groups run (such as run if you have a sister, followed by run if you do not have a sister).

What we have found very successful and motivating is to give students note cards and have them write one or two statements or questions on each side of a card. We then read the cards and the students respond accordingly. This option gives the students the feel that this is their game. One note of caution. Always reserve the right not to use certain statements (such as run if you hate school, or run if you don't like your step dad). Also, students sometimes come up with statements that only apply to a very limited group of people (such as run if you were born in Tallinn, Estonia). You need to determine which of the statements to eliminate. Additional cues can be added at any time. You can build an encyclopedia of information during the school year.

This is a simple game, yet it offers endless possibilities and variations. Variations could include facts and statements related to classroom work.

Competitive and Cooperative Features

This game offers both competitive and cooperative features. To remain in the game as long as possible without getting caught or to catch as many people as possible are obvious competitive features. Dodging, changing directions, and escaping can all be motivating to students who enjoy competition. Getting back into the game after being tagged should also be a goal of the students. Attempting to catch the fastest or most clever runners in class can also add to the competitive nature of the game.

Rescuing others, teaming up with another chaser to trap runners, helping classmates see safe or clear running lanes can add to the qualities of cooperation. Allowing as many students as possible to have the opportunity to be a chaser adds to the quality of this game. Furthermore, writing good running questions or statements adds additional pride or ownership to the game.

Safety Tips

1. Do not allow sliding.
2. Do not allow students to jump over sitting students.
3. Keep your goal lines away from problem areas.
4. Remind students that a tag is a touch. Keep tagging safe.
5. Remind students that runners will be running in both directions so they should be aware of other runners.

Teaching Tips

1. Runners should respond to a cue within three seconds of the call.
2. Chasers should return to a designated area before each cue is given.
3. Students must commit themselves to the fairness policy of accepting a tagger's declaration of a tag.
4. Make it a policy to have as many different chasers as possible.

5. You may wish to discuss safety issues regarding students running in two directions. Be sure your students are taught safe running strategies.

Adaptations

Since this game is an adaptation of Color Tag, refer to the adaptations under that title. In addition, you could make specific adaptations such as relating statements to geography, family history, or family experiences.

Once the basic format of this game has been learned, you can create additional ways for sitting students to reenter the game. One way would be to allow a sitting student to reenter the action if the sitter tags a running chaser. Another way would be to allow a sitting student to reenter after sitting out three consecutive calls. Yet another would be to have designated rescue runners who can tag sitting students with a foam Frisbee. We recommend that any time sitting students reenter the game, they be given free passage to one of the goal lines, they cannot be tagged on their way back into the game.

FROZEN TAG

Lesson Objectives

Frozen Tag is a running game in which running, changing directions, and dodging are very important. This game also allows students to demonstrate their agility, body control, and spatial awareness. Another focus of this game is helping classmates get back into the action once they get caught by the designated chasers.

Grade Range

This game can be played by any grade level.

Activity Area

A space the size of a basketball court is adequate for this game. The shape of the play area could also be a large square.

Equipment Needed

Each student will need a rip flag belt and one rip flag. In addition, you will need approximately six jerseys of one color for the chasers. If you play the game outdoors, you may also need cones for boundary lines.

Activity Description

Each student will stand in a personal space with one rip flag on a rip flag belt. The flag should hang over one hip. Randomly choose six chasers (see figure 5.8). Give each chaser a colored jersey to wear. The chasers drop their flags on the floor. The number of chasers you eventually use will depend on the number of students in your class as well as the skill level of the group.

Chasers will attempt to rip the flags off the runners. The chasers will drop the captured flags onto the floor. If a runner steps out of bounds, the runner must drop his or her flag. Once caught, the runners must stand in the frozen position, that is, feet apart, hands on hips or behind the back. The people caught cannot move their legs or feet.

Runners who have not been caught will try to rescue their classmates. To do so, a runner will pick up a flag, crawl between the feet of a frozen student, and then hand the student a flag. The frozen person must first put the flag on his or her belt before running again.

Chasers may rip off the flags of runners at any time, there are no safe places. Therefore, a student crawling to rescue a friend may be caught, a student putting on a flag may also be caught, no one may ask the chaser to wait while he or she gets ready.

Play the game for either a specific time or until all the runners have been caught.

Competitive and Cooperative Features

Running games usually are motivating and intrinsically competitive. Students being chased want to keep from getting caught and chasers want to catch as many people as possible. These two factors will create competitiveness within the structure of the game. The chasers will also want to catch the entire class as fast as possible.

Figure 5.8 Frozen Tag.

Cooperatively, the students being chased will see the value in rescuing their teammates. Not only is it fun, but keeping more runners active, makes the chasers' role more difficult, and those being chased keep active longer.

The chasers, on the other hand, hopefully will see that by working together, they can isolate runners, catch them, and make rescues more difficult. The fewer the runners, the easier the task of the chasers.

Safety Tips

1. Do not allow any type of holding or tackling.
2. Flags may not be wrapped around a belt.
3. Flags may not be tucked into clothing.
4. Students rescuing classmates must crawl in one specific direction (such as front to back) so that two runners do not bump heads while going under a frozen runner.
5. Keep boundary lines away from walls. You do not want a student who is rescuing a teammate to bump into a wall.
6. Since runners will be running in all directions, be sure to teach the students safe running procedures before playing this game.

Adaptations

Determine the optimum number of chasers for this game. The number will vary due to class size and skill level of the class. You may also create additional ways for frozen students to be rescued.

There are times when the teacher will assist chasers in catching runners if the chasers are having trouble. You may wish to have spy chasers, chasers not identified by jerseys.

Special Comments

This is a vigorous game, especially for the chasers; be sure they do not go too long without a rest. Change the chasers often.

GEEFS AND WEEBLES

Lesson Objectives

This game reinforces the skills of running and dodging as well as body control and agility. A primary focus of this game will be to rescue classmates in order to allow them to quickly get back into the flow of the game. This game combines cooperative and competitive qualities.

Grade Range

This activity can be played in grade 3 and above.

Activity Area

A basketball court-sized area provides adequate space for this game. Since this game can be played indoors as well as outdoors, an area of at least 35' × 60' should be set up outdoors.

Equipment Needed

Each student will need two rip flags and one rip flag belt. Marking cones could be used for outdoor boundary lines.

Activity Description

The names used in this game are strictly nonsensical. Feel free to make any changes that suit your purposes.

Select two students to be the chasers (the Flobs).

Randomly divide the class into two relatively equal groups (the Geefs and the Weebles). As an example, all students with an odd-numbered birth date would be the Geefs and all students with an even-numbered birth date would be the Weebles.

When the Flobs call out, "Geefs," "Weebles," or "Geefs and Weebles," the students representing those groups run across the activity area to the opposite goal line (see figure 5.9).

If a chaser rips off a flag of a runner, the runner must temporarily sit down on his or her seat with legs crossed. The Flobs will drop the captured flags to the floor. If a runner accidentally drops or rips off his or her own flag, that runner is also considered caught. If you use a side boundary line, the consequence for stepping out of bounds should be for that person to take off one flag and sit down. The same consequence

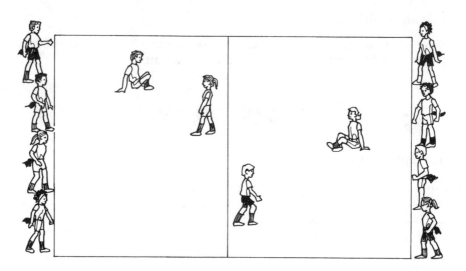

Figure 5.9   Geefs and Weebles.

should be applied to any student sliding in the play area. A student must wear two flags to remain as a runner.

There are two specific ways to get back into the game. One is for a sitting student to rip off the flag of a passing runner. If this happens, the person grabbing the flag gets free passage to one of the goal lines. The person losing the flag sits in the place of the person returning to the goal line. The second method of returning to the game is for a runner to hand a flag to a sitting student. The procedure here is for any student sitting for three or more turns to raise a hand. Any runner may pick up an extra flag off the floor and hand it to the sitting person. The rescued person gets free passage to one of the goal lines.

The Flobs will be working very hard in this game. We suggest changing Flobs frequently. You could use a time limit or a designated number of calls (such as eight) and then change chasers. Additionally, you could start a new game or get new Flobs if they catch a designated number of runners.

Competitive and Cooperative Features

As in most running activities, there is an inherent competitiveness when you have students being chased or being chasers. This game is no exception. Runners will try to keep from getting caught as long as possible. Once caught, they will attempt to get back into the game as quickly as possible. Chasers, on the other hand, will try to catch as many people as possible and try to keep others from rescuing them.

On the cooperative end of this game, runners will hopefully try to rescue classmates whenever possible. The risk factor of trying to rescue someone adds to the competitive, as well as the cooperative, features of Geefs and Weebles. Chasers, naturally, will be more successful if they team together and trap runners in order to catch them.

Safety Tips

1. Do not allow students to slide. They must remain on their feet while running from goal line to goal line.
2. Students rescuing classmates must hand them a flag. If the flag being given to a sitting student touches the floor, the student is not rescued. This helps to keep students in safe positions, and it discourages runners from throwing flags carelessly.

Special Behaviors to Observe

1. Never allow students to wrap a flag around a belt.
2. If students do not sit properly, they cut off safe running paths.

Adaptations

Due to the simplicity of this game, we have not found it necessary to make special adaptations.

Special Comments

You may need to remind students that two flags are necessary to remain as a runner. If a flag falls to the ground, it cannot be put back onto the belt. You may need to encourage students to rescue their classmates. If someone is being ignored, you may have to privately request a specific student rescue that person. If you allow your Flobs to choose their own replacements, be sure they do not conspire to choose at the same time two chasers who might be perceived as the two most ineffective chasers.

NORTH WIND, SOUTH WIND

Lesson Objectives

The focus of this game is to reinforce the skills of running, dodging, changing directions, and safe tagging. Students will also be focusing on strategies that continually bring runners back into the game.

Grade Range

This game can be played at any grade level.

Activity Area

This game can be played indoors as well as outdoors. A basketball court-sized area is adequate for this game. The area can be rectangular or square. You need four distinct boundary lines, one on each side of the play area.

Equipment Needed

You will need three jerseys of one color to represent the North Wind (we usually use black) and one jersey of another color to represent the South Wind (we usually use a striped jersey). If you like to use foam Frisbees for tagging, add them to your list.

Activity Description

Students begin by standing in their individual spaces (see figure 5.10). The South Wind student will wear the yellow jersey and the three North Wind chasers will wear the blue jerseys. The North Wind chasers will attempt to tag as many of the runners as possible. As students are tagged, they sit down or kneel on one knee (make this consequence-specific) in the space where they were tagged.

The South Wind will attempt to tag the students who are in the down position. Once a student is tagged by the South Wind, that student gets up and running again. In addition, the South Wind will try to avoid the North Wind chasers.

Figure 5.10 North Wind, South Wind.

If the South Wind gets tagged, that person must also get down in the designated position. In order for the South Wind to get back into the game, three different runners must tag the South Wind. When the third tag is made, the South Wind gets up running and attempts to rescue the other runners again.

Do not allow the North Wind chasers to stand guard over the South Wind. If fewer than three runners remain, you need to devise a way to rescue the South Wind. One suggestion is to allow a remaining runner to make a tag, then run to a designated area or run around an object such as a circle in the gym, and then make another tag.

Continue the game for a designated time, until all runners are caught, or until a specific number of runners are caught or left.

Competitive and Cooperative Features

This game, like most running games, is naturally competitive. Students being chased usually just run. Chasers chase. Keeping yourself from getting caught or catching as many people as possible are competitive in nature.

Rescuing the South Wind not only requires a cooperative effort, but taking risks in order to rescue the South Wind can be stimulating in a competitive sense. The North Wind people will succeed only if they are either gifted with speed or if they work together cooperatively as a unit.

Safety Tips

1. Always reinforce safe running practices.
2. Do not allow sliding or jumping over classmates.
3. Students in the down position should not be tagged on the head.

Teaching Tips

1. Students must commit to a fairness policy of accepting a tagger's declaration that he or she made a successful tag. Additionally, students must not get back into the game if they were not properly tagged.
2. North Wind chasers may not intentionally stand guard over the South Wind. They must allow a reasonable opportunity for the South Wind to be rescued.

Adaptations

You may wish to add an additional North Wind or an additional South Wind student once the basic format of the game is taught.

Special Comments

This is a very vigorous game for the North and South Wind students. Change their roles often.

BEANBAG BALL

Lesson Objectives

This game can be used as a conditioning exercise. It helps develop strength and agility.

Grade Range

Beanbag Ball is suitable for all grades.

Activity Area

This game is best played outdoors. A large open area is needed. If you play the game indoors, you will need a very large gym to accommodate all the individual courts.

Equipment Needed

You will need beanbags for half of the class plus one hula hoop for each class member. Circles will need to be made by mowing the grass or creating circles with ropes (or tape if indoors).

Activity Description

Divide the class into groups of two. Each group will have a circle set up as seen in figure 5.11. Place the hoops about 10 to 15 yards apart on the field. Mark a circle about 15 feet in diameter and place the hoops directly in the middle of the circle. No other markings will be necessary unless

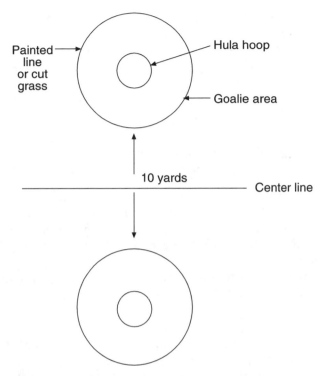

Make enough of these courts for all groups. Or make groups larger — three or four on a team — so that fewer courts will be needed.

Figure 5.11   Beanbag Ball.

you play the game indoors. If played indoors, you should mark boundary lines to keep the courts separate.

The objective of this game is to put the beanbag into one's own hoop without entering the circle around the hoop. The player with the beanbag will attempt to toss the beanbag into the hoop from anywhere outside the circumference of the circle. The area between the hoop and the circumference of the circle is considered the goalie area.

The offensive player will attempt to make a goal by tossing the beanbag into his or her goal. The defensive player will attempt to stop the goal from being scored by catching the beanbag or retrieving a missed toss. The defensive player may step into the goalie area, but not into the hoop.

If a goal is scored or the defensive player gets the beanbag, the players immediately exchange roles, and the person with the beanbag becomes the offensive player and attempts to score a goal in his or her own hoop.

When a goal is scored, the defensive person immediately picks up the beanbag and runs to the opposite goal area. Play should be continuous.

A player does not have to wait for an opponent to get into a ready position before attempting to score a goal.

Defensive players may not tackle or physically steal the beanbag from their opponents. They may, however, intercept a toss or recover a dropped beanbag.

Players may keep track of their own score. The game can be played for a predetermined time or score total before changing courts or opponents.

Competitive and Cooperative Features

This game is designed to be a competitive game with a great deal of continuous movement. Students will be playing against one another and trying to create strategies for outscoring their opponents.

If teammates are added, they will need to cooperate with one another to develop scoring opportunities and to change positions frequently.

There must be a mutual respect for the rule that opponents may not physically touch one another.

Safety Tips

1. Put the courts far enough apart to prevent students from entering the courts of others.
2. Do not allow defensive players to physically touch an opponent.

Teaching Tips

1. Allow students to help determine the optimum distance between goals.
2. Encourage long shots or risk-taking shots at the goal to keep the play of the game continuous.

Adaptation

1. The game can be played with three or four to a team.
2. If multiple players are on a team, require a specific number of passes before a goal can be scored.
3. If space is at a premium and you need to have more students on a team, create a midline and require a certain number of students play on each side of the field. Defenders of one team must pass to the offensive players of their own team.

KICK BALL 300

Kick Ball 300 is a simple, yet effective variation of the old standard playground game of 500. In this activity, students will cooperate with one another in order to give each other turns at kicking as well as pitching and catching. The skills of kicking, catching, and rolling (pitching) will be used and reinforced.

Lesson Objectives

Students take turns playing different positions, pitching to teammates, kicking, and catching. The activity is designed for the students to be rewarded for cooperation among their group. The groups that pitch and kick well will be able to rotate more quickly, which allows for more turns to be taken by each group member.

Grade Range

This activity is suitable for third grade and above.

Activity Area

This activity is designed to be an outdoor activity unless you have a very large indoor area. We suggest that you use the center of a large play area and create a design that looks like a wheel with spokes going out from the center of the circle (see figure 5.12). A soccer or football field is an adequate space.

Equipment Needed

For each group you will need one kick ball, one base, a marking cone, and one poly spot or additional base for the pitcher's area. Groups should consist of four or five students.

Activity Description

Students will be put into groups of four or five. Each group needs one kicker, one pitcher, and two or three fielders. The pitcher is to pitch the ball smoothly to the kicker. It should be an expectation of this activity that the pitcher is attempting to help the kicker be successful. The kicker attempts to kick the ball to the fielders (or pitcher). The students receiving the ball are to try and catch the ball so that they receive a certain number of points:

- A fly ball is worth 100 points.
- A ball caught on one bounce equals 75 points.
- A ball caught on two bounces is worth 50 points.
- Any other rolling ball is worth 25 points.
- A missed ball or dead ball equals zero points.

The fielding group accumulates 300 points as a group (that is, they add their points together). When 300 points are accumulated the group rotates positions. Each student will take a turn at each of the designated positions. You need to reinforce the idea that the kickers should try to kick the ball to their teammates, not just as far as possible.

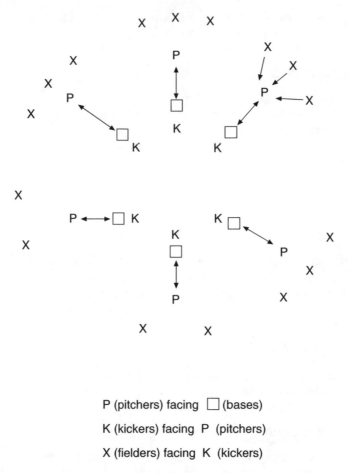

P (pitchers) facing ☐ (bases)

K (kickers) facing P (pitchers)

X (fielders) facing K (kickers)

Figure 5.12   Kick Ball 300.

Additionally, students will be rewarded with more turns as a result of their cooperation.

Competitive and Cooperative Features

Kicking and pitching usually are motivating activities in themselves. To kick and pitch well can be competitive for many students. Trying to succeed at being a person who can kick the ball to his or her teammates and have them accumulate 300 points quickly results in the group developing a nice sense of cooperation. If the fielders adjust to the kicking distance of the kicker, the kicker receives pleasure in kicking the ball both far and accurately.

By changing positions, having everyone contribute to the scoring, and getting multiple kicking turns, the group should keep very active and maintain a high level of cooperation. The success of the group results in the success of individuals, and the success of individuals can result in the success of the group.

Safety Tips

If the student groups are set up so that they are not kicking toward other groups, safety should not be an issue. The use of Nerf-type soccer balls reduces the chances of getting hurt by a missed catch, and this type of ball does not travel as far as a playground-type ball.

Teaching Tips

When introducing this activity, the kickers may need encouragement in order to get them to kick the ball toward their teammates. Pitchers need to understand that good pitching increases the success level of the kickers. If kickers do not attempt to kick the ball toward the fielders, the fielders will become frustrated or discouraged. Encouraging the kickers to kick the ball so that the fielders quickly accumulate points results in rapid changing of positions, which in turn keeps the group highly motivated.

Adaptations

The point system used here is both arbitrary and traditional. Feel free to change the values attached to certain types of catches. If time is running short in your class, students could kick a specified number of kicks rather than having the fielders accumulate points. As an example, after each student has had a kicking turn to 300 points, each would get five kicks on his or her second turn. The fielders could see how many points they could accumulate on each kicker. No matter how many points were scored, students would rotate after five kicks (one kicker could kick five fly balls for 500 points).

INDY 500

Lesson Objective

This lesson, using scooters, combines teamwork and role changing along with a strenuous cardiovascular workout.

Grade Range

This activity can be done in grades 4 through 8.

Activity Area

A basketball court-sized area will be necessary. This is primarily an indoor activity.

Equipment Needed

The students will be divided into groups of three. Each group will need one scooter. You will need approximately twenty cones to make an oval track (see figure 5.13). You will also need one or two tumbling mats. A note card and pencil should be supplied to each group. A stopwatch may be used.

Activity Description

Using the cones, build an oval track within the basketball court area. Allow enough space between the cones and any outside wall to permit three or four scooters to pass safely. Unfold the mats and set them inside the track.

Each group should station themselves near a cone, which will be used as their marking cone for completed laps around the track. You may

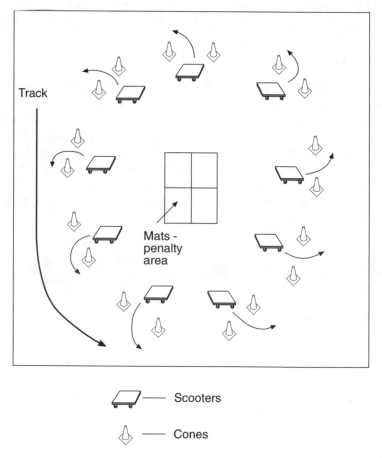

Figure 5.13   Indy 500.

wish to have each group choose a racing name such as Team Toyota, Cruising Corvettes, Boss Mustangs, and so forth. Each group should choose a racing order for the team members.

The first person can be the driver, the second person the mechanic, and the third person the crew chief. The driver will ride the scooter, the mechanic will push the driver, and the crew chief will record lap information or track infractions on the note card. At the completion of each lap, the three teammates quickly rotate positions and tasks.

As the Indy 500 begins, each team completes one lap around the track. They immediately continue another lap after the group members switch places. The goal is to complete as many laps as possible in a given time period or to time themselves for a specific number of laps.

During the race there also will be a track patrol, either the teacher or a designated number of students (two or three). The track patrol will be on the lookout for track safety infractions such as the following:

1. The driver falls off the scooter.
2. The mechanic pushes too hard and loses contact with the driver.
3. A race team runs into another team (fender bender).
4. Cones are hit by the race teams.
5. A race team touches a wall.
6. The students use last names when speaking to other students.
7. The students use put-downs or impolite behavior during the race.

When the track patrol witnesses an infraction, penalties such as the following can be imposed: added time to the race team's accumulative race time, deductions of successful lap points, or the red flag, which sends the team to the mat inside the track for a special assignment or penalty time period.

An alternative challenge may be to run a specific number of laps accident free.

The changing of positions could take place inside the track. As a driving team completes a lap they enter the track by coming inside the left hand side of their marking cone. After the switch of positions, they go back onto the track passing their cone with the cone on their right hand side.

Competitive and Cooperative Features

Groups will be competing against each other as they complete laps either by time or total laps. There will be cooperative efforts taking place among teammates. Safe pushing will be chief among the cooperative needs. A good strategy of pushing rotation should be demonstrated.

Lap results could be accumulative for the class. That is, the teacher could set a group challenge rather than individual competitions. Teams could be acknowledged for safe driving.

Teaching Tips

1. You may wish to create a pit stop area where teams enter the inside of the track and exit back onto the track at specific places.
2. The note cards could be used to record successful laps as well as penalty points.
3. Teams could be numbered or wear colored jerseys for easier identification.
4. If helmets are available, they could be worn by the drivers.
5. As the driver is being pushed by the mechanic, the mechanic must keep both hands on the driver for the entire lap.

Adaptations

1. Allow the use of additional scooters if students need them to ride safely. One scooter would be to sit upon and the other would be placed under the legs.
2. Wave the yellow caution flag for short rest periods if needed.

WALL BALL

Lesson Objective

This game will provide hand–eye coordination skill practice as well as provide students with a good source of exercise and competition.

Grade Range

By using different sizes or types of balls, this game can be adapted for grades 5 and above.

Activity Area

A flat wall space in the gym or outdoors will be necessary. An area 20 to 30 feet from the wall will also be needed. Each pair or group of students will need their own small court approximately 10 to 12 feet wide.

Equipment Needed

One ball per set of students will be needed. The size or type of ball can be determined by age or skill level. As an example, playground balls might be used by younger students, while tennis balls might be used by older or more skilled players. Tape or chalk will be used to mark court lines.

Activity Description

Set up the courts as shown in figure 5.14. Court size will depend somewhat on your facility size. You may be able to create courts larger than shown.

The student starting the game must stand behind the serving line. The serving student bounces the ball and hits it against the wall on the fly, the ball must then rebound across the return line. The receiving student must catch the ball in the air after it hits the wall or after one bounce. After the receiver catches the ball, the ball must immediately be thrown against the wall. The serving student must then move to catch the ball in the air or on one bounce. The process continues until one person does not catch the ball. Points are scored by the server. If a receiver wins a volley, that person then becomes the server (similar to the process in volleyball, handball, or racquetball). All serves must be from behind the serving line.

Rules can be added or altered to fit the needs of your class. Some suggestions include the following:

- If the receiver misses or fumbles the ball, a point is scored by the server. If the opposite occurs, the receiver wins the right to serve.
- If the thrower's ball is thrown out of bounds or does not make it past the return line, the other person either scores a point or wins the serve.
- Any ball that hits a line is considered in bounds.

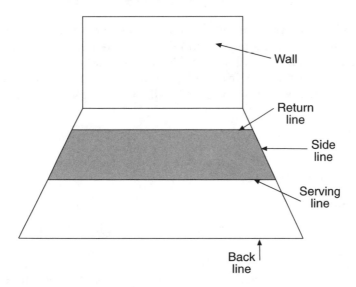

Figure 5.14 Wall Ball.

- If a player gets in the way of his or her opponent, a hinder is called and the volley is replayed.

Competitive and Cooperative Features

Playing singles can be very competitive. This game depends on opponents to also be partners, in that playing together increases the time on task as well as the enjoyment of playing the game. A cooperative feature may be trying to complete a certain number of wall passes or progressively moving farther and farther away from the wall.

Safety Tips

1. Keep enough space between courts to allow students room to play safely.
2. Use a ball that will not hurt students when caught.
3. Consider ability levels when grouping students.

Adaptations

1. Allow multiple bounces for students having difficulty catching the ball.
2. Require throws to hit a smaller target on the wall.
3. Teach doubles or cutthroat (groups of three with students rotating two against one).

FOOTBALL PASSING GAME

The Football Passing Game was created to solve a problem we sometimes have in Minnesota: we don't know when we can be outdoors during many of the months due to changing weather conditions, so we need indoor activities. Additionally, we wanted to find a way to utilize some skills related to the use of footballs without playing a traditional football game.

Lesson Objectives

The students will use and reinforce the skills of throwing, catching, and, hopefully, catching a ball while moving.

Grade Range

This game can be played by third grade through high school.

Activity Area

Although this game was designed to be played indoors, it certainly can be played outdoors. Typically, the game is played using a basketball court-sized area. If larger spaces are available, it simply allows for more options for running patterns as well as allowing for greater throwing distances.

Originally, this game was designed for two teams. However, if enough space is available, more teams can play at the same time. For the sake of this explanation, we will assume two teams are to be playing at one time.

Equipment Needed

Each team will need one Itza-type football (an inflatable type rubber football that has good surface texture), one deck tennis ring, one marking cone, one tumbling mat or crash pad (if game is played near a wall space), and a scorecard usable by both teams. You may also need some marking tape to mark a few lines on the floor for starting areas.

Activity Description

The two teams will be placed in two lines behind tape marks, in opposite corners of the gymnasium from one another (see figure 5.15). One tape mark will be designated the passers' line and the other tape mark, the receivers' line. We recommend that the tape marks be different colors.

The footballs will be set on the deck tennis rings near the middle of the playing space. You may wish to make a tape mark for the rings because they will be moved during the course of play. Set the footballs far enough apart so that students running toward them do not run into one another.

The passers' line should be set diagonally facing the center of the gymnasium or play area. The receivers' line will be set so that the

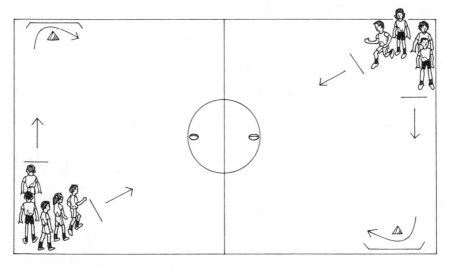

Figure 5.15   Football Passing Game.

runners will run across the basketball court area toward the marking cone. If the cone is near a wall space, stand a tumbling mat or crash pad against the wall to protect students from running into the wall.

The teacher will give a signal (such as a hand clap). On that signal, one passer from each team runs to the team's ball, picks it up, and prepares to throw the ball to the team's receiver. The receiver may not start running until the passer touches the ball.

The passer will attempt to throw the ball to the receiver as the receiver runs across the gym toward the cone. If the receiver catches the ball, he or she runs around the cone, back to the deck tennis ring set near the center of the basketball court, and sets the ball on the ring.

Students will score points in the following manner: if a ball is caught, one point is automatically scored by either or both receivers. Additionally, the first receiver to catch the ball and replace it on the ring will receive a bonus point. No point can be scored if the ball is not caught. Ties are worth two points each. So a receiver can score two, one, or zero points per turn.

As soon as a passer and receiver complete their turn, they return to their team, but they switch lines, so that each will do the opposite task the next time his or her turn comes up. Often times, we have the person who scores points first, run to the scorecard, add the points, then return to the correct line.

In order for this game to be most effective, the students must be taught the pattern of movement for the game so that the game moves very rapidly. Once the students have learned this pattern, try to clap your hands every 6–8 seconds.

If a student does not catch the ball, he or she immediately retrieves the ball and returns it to the ring.

Once you have gone through the pattern of movement a few times, the game moves very fast.

Competitive and Cooperative Features

This game is always fun and exciting. Students do compete as they attempt to catch the ball and run back to the ring in order to score points. Returning to the ring first is rewarded by bonus points. Trying to accumulate lots of points does encourage competition.

The cooperative features include the need to encourage each teammate as they pass and attempt to catch the ball. Students who are good throwers need to be encouraged to throw catchable passes. If the ball is thrown too hard, it cannot be caught, and a missed pass results in zero points. Adopting the methods mentioned in the special comments section seems to create a very pleasant attitude toward the game.

As in all games, when students make mistakes (and we should expect the mistakes) they need encouragement, not disparaging words. We rarely, if ever, have heard one person thank another for pointing out the fact that he or she missed or dropped the ball.

It is very possible to create an atmosphere in your class where students do not fear making an error or mistake.

Safety Tips

1. As previously mentioned, you may need to set a tumbling mat against a wall space if a cone is set near a wall.
2. Set the deck tennis rings far enough apart so that passers do not bump into each other.
3. It is common for receivers racing back to the rings to attempt to slide on the floor in order to be the first one back. Do not allow this.
4. Caution receivers not to dive to catch a ball on the gym floor.

Teaching Tips

Have one or two groups demonstrate the patterns of movement before starting the game.

Adaptations

As we said earlier, you can use more than two teams if your space allows for it. You might have to change the scoring system.

The placement of the deck tennis rings could call for certain adaptations. If the throwing area is too far for some students, allow them to move forward. You might wish to mark a throwing line. Some gymnasium floors happen to be marked with a large circle. You could ask your students to throw from within that circle, or choose an area as needed.

Special Comments

In order to discourage yelling and loud behaviors, ask your students to clap for every successful catch or good effort. For every missed pass or fumble, suggest that they grab their head and say "Oooh" or kneel down and pound the floor in mock disappointment. Usually both responses add to the humor of the game and to the enjoyment of the game if the class is good-natured.

NET BALL VOLLEYBALL

Lesson Objectives

The purpose of this activity is to reinforce the skills of serving, bumping, passing, and receiving a volleyball. In addition, students will be catching the ball.

Grade Range

This activity is designed for grades 3 through 7. With adaptations or rule changes, the game can be played by older students.

Activity Area

A minimum of two volleyball courts is necessary. If more courts are available, it will allow for fewer players on a team, which is desirable. This game can be played indoors or outdoors.

Equipment Needed

You will need at least one training (lightweight) volleyball per court plus volleyball standards and nets.

Activity Description

The game consists of hitting the volleyball over the net with a serve, bump, or set. If a player is able to put the ball over the net without it being caught by the opposing team, a point is scored by that individual. If the ball touches the floor in bounds, a point is awarded to the person hitting the ball over the net. If the ball is caught, no point is scored.

The person catching the ball immediately sends the ball back over the net using a serve, set, or bump. Each person keeps track of his or her individual score. You have the option of rotating positions every time the ball is caught or rotating every 60 seconds.

In this description, not everyone will get an equal chance to hit the ball over the net.

Competitive and Cooperative Features

Competitively, in this description, each student will be his or her own team, scoring individual points. If team scoring is used, one team will be attempting to outscore the other.

Cooperatively, if team scoring is used or if passing to teammates is rewarded with points, the better a student bumps and sets the ball, the easier it will be for others to successfully hit the ball.

In all cases, students need to be committed to respect the space or positions of the players on their side of the net. Infringing on the space of others could cause students to run into one another or cause teammates to hesitate when attempting to hit the ball.

Safety Tips

1. The positions of others must be respected by the team players, otherwise students will collide or get in each other's way when trying to catch the ball.

2. If necessary, divide each court into six to eight receiving areas. A player could only catch a ball that came into his or her area.

Teaching Tips

1. If needed, lower the net for younger players.
2. Encourage students to attempt to hit the ball immediately after they catch it to keep a fast pace to the game.
3. Students call out individual scores each time one hits the ball over the net.

Adaptations

1. You can add volleyballs to the game and have more than one ball in play at a time.
2. You can change the scoring system in a variety ways. One way would be to give two points for a back row hit and one point for a front row hit. Another is to give one point for a serve, two for a set, and three for a bump that goes over the net and is not caught.
3. A point could be awarded for a catch.
4. Teams could accumulate scores.
5. Teams could be given points for receiving a ball with a bump or set, then a catch.
6. Teams could receive a point for each consecutive set or bump when receiving the ball.

TENNIS BASEBALL

Lesson Objectives

The students will become more skilled using the forehand and backhand tennis strokes.

Grade Range

This activity is suitable for sixth through ninth grades.

Activity Area

Tennis courts will be needed for this activity. The more courts you have available, the smaller the groups you can form, and the more practice time each student will receive.

Equipment Needed

Five tennis balls, three hula hoops, and one racquet per court will be needed.

Activity Description

Each tennis court will be divided into halves. One half will be the batting half and the other, the fielding half (see figure 5.16). The fielding half of the court will need to be marked into scoring areas. Specific areas for singles, doubles, triples, and home runs will need to be designated.

For the description of this activity, we will assume there are six students at each court.

The offensive team consists of two batters and a pitcher. The defensive team consists of three players, each inside a hula hoop. The hoops cannot be moved, nor can a defensive player move out of a hoop to catch a ball. Please note that the hoops could be moved at the beginning of an inning, but not after play has begun or during the inning.

The pitcher (part of the offensive or batting team) must pitch the ball to a batter using a one-bounce toss. The batter stands behind the end service line with the tennis racquet. The batter will attempt to hit the pitched ball into the scoring areas across the net. The batter does not run any bases, but attempts to put runners on base (imaginary runners on imaginary bases). After hitting the ball, the batter becomes the pitcher, the pitcher moves to await a turn at bat, and the batter waiting his or her turn (on deck) takes a turn to hit. The new pitcher pitches the ball and the new batter attempts to get a fair ball hit. Hitters advance runners when hitting the ball into scoring areas. The batting team will continue hitting until they accumulate three outs.

The defensive team players will try to get the batters out by catching the hit balls while remaining inside the hoops. Outs are also received if the ball is hit into the net or hit out of bounds. Once three outs are accumulated, the two teams switch places and responsibilities.

Using multiple tennis balls keeps the game moving. Students do not have to retrieve a ball each time a ball is hit.

Competitive and Cooperative Features

By allowing the batting team to provide the pitcher, the toss is likely to be very hittable. However, the competitive aspect of the game is much like baseball, the more runs scored, the better your chances of winning the game.

Competition can be reduced by taking the defensive players out of the game: eliminate the hoops and have the defense simply retrieve the tennis balls until it becomes their turn to bat.

Runs could be accumulated by both teams during the class period rather than score being kept separately.

An additional cooperative activity could be added. The defensive team (if playing in the hoops) could have to throw the ball to each team member after one of them caught the ball in order to record an out.

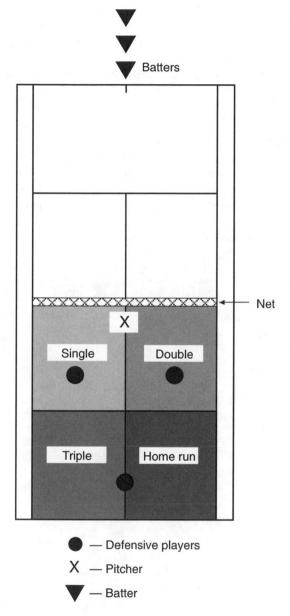

Figure 5.16   Tennis Baseball.

Safety Tips

1. Make sure that the on deck batter or hitter is not close to the person who is considered at bat.
2. Pitchers must be prepared to get out of the way of batted (hit) balls.

Teaching Tips

1. Make sure the students are using a correct hitting grip when striking the ball.
2. Allow the tosser or pitcher to use either overhand or underhand pitches.

Adaptations

1. You could have students run bases.
2. You could alternate the types of strokes the hitters use, such as forehand one inning and backhand the next inning.
3. You could use time limits per hitting turn as well as maximum runs per inning in order to ensure both teams relatively equal hitting turns.
4. Allow only one pitch per student per turn.

PACING LESSON I

Teaching students to pace themselves is an important lesson often overlooked when teaching the skills related to running. Since many physical education programs utilize the mile run or nine-minute run as an indicator of endurance, students have an advantage if they learn how to pace themselves while running.

Lesson Objectives

The purpose of this activity is to teach the concept of pacing while running.

Grade Range

This activity can be taught to grade 4 and above.

Activity Area

Use a space the area of a regular basketball court. You will make an oval track approximately 50 meters in perimeter. This activity can be done indoors or outdoors. We recommend teaching this lesson first indoors. You will have fewer distractions and the activity is more easily monitored than when teaching outside.

Equipment Needed

Fourteen cones will be used to make your track. Each student will need one pencil and one worksheet. One stopwatch or timer will be used. Some vinyl tape may be needed to mark two starting lines if you cannot use existing lines on the floor (see figure 5.17). Pulse monitors are a valuable addition to this lesson if you have them available.

Activity Description

Build a track approximately 50 meters in perimeter, for example, just inside the basketball court of your gym space, if you have a court. The size of the track should allow you to jog around it comfortably in 15 seconds. Create two starting lines opposite one another on the track. These lines also serve as lap markers and finish lines.

Have the students work with a recording partner. One student will run in group one and the other student will run in group two.

Before having the students begin their running activity, demonstrate the pace necessary to jog around the track in exactly 15 seconds. You could have them time you, or choose a dependable student to jog.

As the students in group one get onto the track, have half of them start on one side of the track and the other half at the opposite starting line on the track. Their recording partners should be prepared with a pencil and the runner's worksheet (see appendix).

Direct the runners to run together as a group, to stay close like a bunch of bananas or grapes, as they attempt to jog the track in exactly 15 seconds. When crossing the finish line, they should not stop, but rather jog beyond the line a few yards or meters so as not to create a traffic jam.

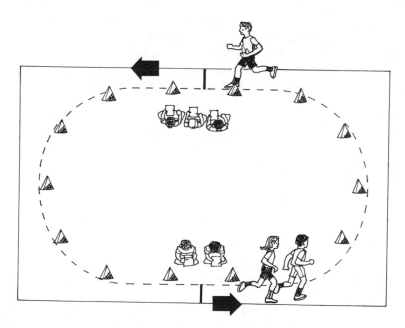

Figure 5.17   Pacing Lesson I.

The recording partner should record in the first box on the worksheet the number of seconds it takes the runner to jog around the track. In order to assist the runners and recorders, call out loud the number of seconds while the runners are running. This serves to help the recorders, but also gives the runners cues for proper pace.

You may wish to have each group try a practice lap while you count out the fifteen seconds just to give them a feel for the pace at which they will be running. Do not be concerned if the students say the pace is way too slow.

After the practice lap has occurred, and you start the activity with one lap, the students in group one will jog their lap and the recorders will write the times on the worksheet. You will then have the students switch places and repeat the first lap directions with group two students jogging the track.

Upon completion of group two's lap, record the results and put group one back onto the track. Group one will be jogging twice around the track on this turn. Their goal is to run two laps at 15 seconds each. They will listen for cues of 15 seconds for the first lap and try to cross the finish line at exactly 30 seconds on the second lap. The recording partner needs to record the running partner's time at each lap interval. Have the groups switch places and tasks. Continuing to use the worksheets, groups will jog three laps (15, 30, and 45 seconds as target times) and then four laps (15, 30, 45, and 60 seconds as target times).

During the lesson, even though you will be calling out the seconds, give encouragement to the groups to stay together. There is no extra credit for finishing first. In fact, it is very common for the first finishers to be way too fast. The more the group members become separated from one another, the less likely they are to achieve the objective of the lesson.

Hopefully, you will still have time to continue with the next activity.

Have each group experiment with a new lap speed. They will set their own goal. We recommend that students choose a lap time from 12–18 seconds (but not 15 seconds). Times of less than 12 seconds diminish the likelihood of runners properly pacing themselves, while times of more than 18 seconds take too long and reduce the challenge of staying on task. Have each group attempt to jog one lap at their chosen lap speed.

Next, have the students write the first four multiples of their chosen lap speed on the worksheet. Each group will attempt to jog four laps and reach their goals while the recording partners write down the time at each lap interval.

Collect the worksheets at the end of class. They can be used for student portfolios or as the basis of discussion on pacing or setting reasonable goals.

Competitive and Cooperative Features

This lesson is not designed to be a competitive one. However, there will be many students who will have a built-in desire or sense that being on the goal numbers is as successful as winning. That is just fine, we want the students to take pride in their performance.

There is a need in this lesson for the runner to cooperate with his or her recording partner in order to report accurate information. Additionally, the students who cooperate with one another as they jog as a group usually enjoy continuous success and find this lesson helpful and interesting.

Safety Tips

Usually this lesson does not present safety problems. However, remind students to be careful while running in close proximity with their group members. Bumping others could cause a fall.

Teaching Tips

1. To fit this entire lesson into a 30-minute class period requires good planning and very effective use of time. As soon as one group is done with their part of the lesson, the next group must immediately get on the track.
2. Recording partners need to pay close attention to the runners as they cross the finish line.
3. Remember to encourage groups to try to keep together as they attempt to meet the pacing goal.
4. Sometimes it helps to give students a visual cue such as raising your hand when they are within one second of the goal or right on the goal number (such as raising your hand while counting "14, 15, 16").
5. You can be certain that you will have students who run fast and come almost to a complete stop while jogging in place in order to cross the line on the goal number. Conversely, you will have students who jog too slow and then speed up hurriedly in order to make the time goal. In both cases, point out that they may be crossing the line at the correct moment, but they are not pacing themselves correctly.
6. For some groups, it is helpful to discuss their first half-lap time. A pace faster than seven seconds means the pace is too fast, while hearing numbers of eight or more means the pace is too slow. In both cases, the group needs to make adjustments.

Adaptations

1. Adapt the size of the track to meet your students' needs.

2. If there are students having a harder time keeping on pace, allow them to shorten the distance by having them run just inside the cones.
3. Set walking goals if you have students who are unable to jog.

Special Comments

If you have heart monitors, use them. You may also try having the students reach heart-rate levels rather than concern yourself with keeping the groups together. However, we feel that teaching this lesson before using the heart-monitor feedback will help to teach the concept of running under control.

This lesson is designed to teach a concept rather than deal exclusively with individual differences. By working together in the small groups, students will help one another stay on task and reach the goals as a group. This in turn should reinforce the concept of pacing for your entire class. There will be those students begging to run faster.

Often different classes exhibit unusual and sometimes humorous ways to create motivation during the class period. We have had groups who get a lot of humor out of jumping in the air or throwing their hands up high if they are right on the goal number as they cross the marking lines. Encourage these little demonstrations of fun, they add to the value of student participation in class.

PACING LESSON II

This lesson is a continuation of lesson I. The lesson objectives, grade range, and activity area all remain the same as in lesson I. If you have enough stopwatches for one watch per group of students, you will be able to make good use of them in this lesson. Additionally, if you have lap counters, you will be able to make use of them as well. If you do not have lap counters, you might wish to supply the students with a note card or scrap piece of paper, which they will use in their recording duties. You will also supply the students with a new worksheet (see appendix).

Although the setup for lesson II is the same as lesson I, each pair of students will start by their own marking cone rather than the communal starting line (see figure 5.18).

Activity Description

We will assume that the students participated in lesson I and have an understanding of the mechanics of the pacing lesson.

The students will warm up with four laps using the 15-second lap speed as their goal (use the worksheet). When group one is finished, group two will begin on your signal. However, instead of running

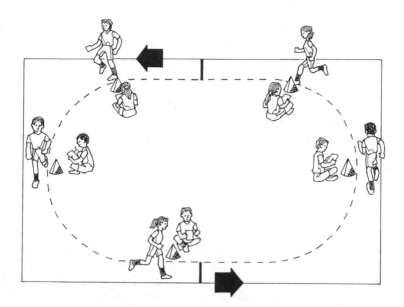

Figure 5.18 Pacing Lesson II.

together in a bunch, each student will jog as an individual not as one of the group.

The next step will be to change the lap speed as was done in lesson I, using 12- to 18-second laps. Each group will run one practice lap before going on to the next step, which is four laps at the chosen speed (such as 13, 26, 39, and 52 seconds, using 13-second laps as an example).

If students wish to change lap speeds because they feel they have under- or overestimated their abilities, no problem. They simply will change numbers on the worksheet and do the correct math.

The following task will require a little discussion on prediction as well as the use of some math skills. The students will be asked to jog for two minutes at their chosen lap speed. They will also be asked to estimate to the nearest one-half lap the number of laps they will complete during this time period. It is important for the recorder to keep an accurate tally of laps during this time. If you have lap counters available, use them. If not, have the recording students use a stick-figure tally system of keeping track of each lap. As the teacher, you will only give them a few cues. The first is the start cue, then you will call out the last five seconds ("1:55, 1:56, . . . 2:00 minutes") so that the recorder can watch carefully for the last few steps. The runner and recorder should agree on an estimate of the nearest quarter- or half-lap, depending on how you wish to deal with fractions. Hopefully, the estimate of laps run during the time period will correspond to the running pace set by the runner. Group two repeats the activity in the same manner as group one.

In the next assignment, it will be helpful to have a stopwatch per set of students; if they are not available, a large clock would work as a substitute. If a clock is not available, you will have to verbally call out times again. Students will estimate how much time it will take to run a certain number of laps using their chosen lap speed. For this example, we will use 12 seconds for the lap speed and 10 laps for the running distance. A student running on pace at 12 seconds a lap should take two minutes and 24 seconds to complete the run (the recorder can write it as 2:24). If recording partners have stopwatches, they can help keep the runners on goal by talking to them or giving them hand signals to speed up or slow down. Again, group two follows group one in performing this part of the lesson. Recorders must count accurately and give undivided attention to the runners.

By now the students have had numerous chances to demonstrate their understanding of the concept of pacing. If time allows, you may wish to repeat a part of either pacing lesson, create a new task, or have the students attempt a five-minute jog using a chosen lap speed. For the increased time, you might wish to encourage the students to reduce their lap speed (anywhere from 12–20 seconds per lap). Again they can estimate the number of laps by using their math skills.

Competitive and Cooperative Features

As in lesson I, there will be motivation to reach individual goals. You may still have some students who feel finishing first wins, but that should diminish quickly. If there is any competition, it will be to see who has consistently met their goal times right on the numbers. Again, this is a nice demonstration of competition.

Cooperatively, group members must work hard for one another. Accurate times and lap counts are expected. Encouragement and praise for each other's efforts should be continually reinforced.

Teaching Tips

1. These lessons were originally designed for 30-minute class periods. It is possible that you might not finish the entire lesson within that time period. Make adjustments as needed. Do not worry about delaying a part of a lesson until the next day. The value of teaching the concept of pacing is worth the time spent.
2. If your class periods are substantially longer than 30 minutes, you may wish to combine the two lessons and delete some of the repeated tasks.
3. If you find this lesson effective, we are sure you can find some new twists to the assignments. Most likely your students can come up with new challenges or estimation problems to solve.

FITNESS DECATHLON

The Fitness Decathlon is a 10-event activity that allows students to attempt to achieve their highest level of performance in a variety of fitness activities. For our discussion, we will use 10 activities, which we chose at random, worth up to 100 points per activity. Fitness Decathlon has many similarities to the next activity, Challenge of the Century.

Lesson Objectives

This activity will provide students with 10 self-testing activities. These activities will allow them to participate in a variety of fitness activities. Students will try to achieve their best possible results; the achievements will be measured by keeping accumulative performance scores.

Grade Range

This activity can be adapted to any grade level.

Activity Area

The fitness decathlon can be done indoors or outdoors. Some components could be completed in the gymnasium facility, while others could be done outdoors. The size area needed will depend on the type of activities you choose to use. However, it is very likely that you will choose 10 different activities that could be done in a basketball court-sized area.

Equipment Needed

Again, your equipment requirements will depend upon your choice of fitness activities. For the examples used in the activity description, the equipment needed will be minimal, and no special equipment will be required.

Activity Description

Students will generally work in partner groups but other small groups, depending on the needs of the students or teacher, could certainly be used. Generally, one student in a set of partners (or small group) will participate in an activity, while the other helps to monitor or count successful responses.

For our discussion we will use the following 10 activities:

1. Curl-ups
2. 10-minute run
3. Shuttle run
4. Rope jumping (long rope)
5. Bent arm hang

6. Push-ups
7. Jumping jacks
8. Pull-ups or chin-ups
9. Rope jumping (short rope)
10. Sit and reach (flexibility test)

Each activity will be worth up to 100 points. Students may earn less, but not more than 100 points in any given activity (see variations). Just how exacting you wish to make the accounting system is up to you. We will give examples for each of the mentioned activities. See the appendix for a sample student evaluation form.

1. **Curl-ups:** Students get one point for each curl-up they are able to do. They will get two, one-minute attempts. They will add their scores together, 100 points maximum.
2. **10-minute run:** Students will attempt to run for 10 consecutive minutes. They will receive 10 points for each minute they complete. You may prorate each minute on a chart if you wish, such as 95 points for nine and one-half minutes.
3. **Shuttle run:** There are two different ways to conduct this challenge. The first is to have the students run consecutive laps across the width of the gym or basketball court, much like the pacer test used with the Fitness Gram. Students get one point for each lap across to the opposite wall or line; 100 laps equals 100 points. A time limit could be used, such as seven minutes.

    The second method is to use a prorated time chart using a shuttle-run test similar to the Presidential Fitness Test. Using a 40-foot shuttle run with two running turns each direction, your time chart might look like the following:

    11.0 seconds = 100 points
    11.1 seconds = 99 points
    11.2 seconds = 98 points, and so forth. You probably would have to create a time chart for the students to read and find their performance scores.
4. **Rope jumping (long rope):** Students will be given a five-minute time limit (an arbitrary number) in which to accumulate the highest number of consecutive jumps, up to 100. Their score would reflect the highest number of consecutive jumps performed during the time trial.
5. **Bent arm hang:** Students will attempt the bent arm hang using either the pull-up or chin-up grip. They would receive one point for each second they keep the chin above the bar.
6. **Push-ups:** Students will attempt to do as many push-ups during a time period (such as two or three minutes) as they can. They

would receive three points per push-up, but would have to do 34 to receive 100 points.

7. **Jumping jacks:** Students will have a two-minute time trial in which to do as many consecutive jumping jacks as possible. They would receive one-half point per jumping jack, 200 jumping jacks equal 100 points.

8. **Pull-ups or chin-ups:** Students will score 10 points per pull-up or chin-up. A reasonable time limit would be provided.

9. **Rope jumping (short rope):** A two-minute time limit will be provided for students to achieve as many jumps as possible. The jumps could be either accumulative (not necessarily in a row) or consecutive; 100 jumps equal 100 points.

10. **Sit and reach:** Students will do the sit and reach test as administered in the Fitness Gram or AAHPERD youth fitness test. Students could achieve 10 points per inch if a standard ruler is used or 2–3 points per centimeter if the metric system is used. A 100 point system could be provided by the teacher.

Competitive and Cooperative Features

The competitiveness found in the Fitness Decathlon will most likely occur in the attempts to achieve the highest scores possible. Hopefully, the activities will allow for self-motivation and desire for self-improvement. There will probably be those who are motivated to compete against the scoring system and those who will be motivated to compete against classmates. You may wish to carefully control the second type of motivation if it presents a negative impact.

Cooperatively, students should be motivated and taught to assist and encourage their working partners. Encouragement can come from anyone in the class and personal improvement in performance should be highly encouraged.

Safety Tips

There are no special directions for safety tips offered here.

Teaching Tips

1. Either provide the students with personal scorecards or collect the scores yourself on a master sheet.

2. You may wish to have students choose their own partners for scorekeeping or personally assign students to work with partners. Either way, the students must make a commitment to honesty and integrity in keeping correct scores.

3. It is your option to have the entire class working on the same challenge at the same time or to set up stations and encourage more self-reliance.

Adaptations

Remember, the 10 items listed for the Fitness Decathlon are for example only. You can create your own list of 10 events. The scoring system is also for example only.

You may wish to have unlimited point accumulations. For example, if a student jumps 307 consecutive jumps with a jump rope, that becomes the student's score. It might be advisable to put a time limit on each of the decathlon events (such as five or 10 minutes), although each activity could have a different time limit.

As a possible motivator, you could set up certain criteria for achievement recognition. Example: if you use a 1,000-point maximum system, 950 or more points could earn a gold medal, 850—the silver medal, 750—the bronze medal, and fewer than 750 points—the recycled plastic award (just kidding).

The Fitness Decathlon could be done periodically during the school year with students being able to raise their achievement scores each succeeding time.

CHALLENGE OF THE CENTURY

One of the four definitions of "century" in Webster's dictionary, is that it means a series, group, or amount of 100 like things. In Challenge of the Century, students will be challenged to complete 100 successes in a variety of skill, activity, or fitness challenges.

Challenge of the Century is similar to the Fitness Decathlon in that you will choose 10 activities that will serve as challenges for the students to complete, or attempt to achieve their highest level of performance. The activities used for Challenge of the Century can be any skills or activities you wish to use that are easily administered in your teaching station.

For the sake of discussion and explanation, we will use 10 different activities, arbitrarily chosen, but also ones that we have used in our classes.

Lesson Objectives

As previously stated, students will be asked to complete a variety of challenges. The goal will be to achieve 100 successful attempts in each of the activities chosen.

Grade Range

This activity can be taught at any grade level.

Activity Area

Although this activity is usually conducted in a gymnasium space, it certainly could be done outdoors. For this explanation, we will consider a basketball court-sized gym space as our activity area.

Equipment Needed

Due to the great variety of possibilities available for this activity, we will not list specific equipment needs. The specific needs will be determined by the choices you make for your own class. However, you will need to provide enough equipment for partners to share as they participate in pairs. For example, if you are doing a throwing and catching challenge, you will need one ball per two students; if you are doing a short rope jumping activity, you might need one rope per student in order to accommodate individual size differences.

As you read through the list of activities we use in our examples, you will note that we mention there the equipment needed.

This activity can be administered in more than one way. All students could participate in the same activity at one time, or you could provide a variety of stations where students work and rotate when their challenges are completed.

Activity Description

The students will work with a partner during the following activities. You may wish to supply the students with a worksheet on which they can record their scores, or you may wish to record the scores on a master list (see the appendix for a sample student evaluation form).

1. **Throw and one bounce catch:** Using a predetermined distance (such as 15–20 feet), the students will stand behind a line facing a wall space. They are expected to throw a playground ball against the wall using a one-handed overhand throw. The ball is to bounce back to the throwing student and they are to catch it on one bounce. The students will be given the assignment to make 100 consecutive catches. If a miss occurs (due to a missed catch, a poor throw, or a situation where the ball bounces more than one time), the student starts the task again. One partner throws while the other helps to keep score. Partners switch tasks upon completion of 100 catches. You will need one ball per set of partners.

2. **Partner toss and catch:** Using a specific type of ball (such as an Itza football or a softball), the partners each throw and catch a ball 100 consecutive times. If a miss occurs, both partners begin the task again. The ball must cross over a minimum, predetermined distance. The maximum distance may be determined by

the width of your teaching space. You will need one ball per set of partners.

3. **Baseball or tennis ball throw and catch:** Using a soft baseball or tennis ball, a student throws the ball against a wall space and catches the rebound, on the fly, 100 consecutive times. The ball must be thrown above a predetermined mark or height on the wall. Students should stand five to 10 feet from the wall. Partners switch tasks after one person completes a turn. You will need one ball per set of partners.

4. **Basket shooting:** Students must make 100 baskets (accumulatively) from a reasonable distance from a basket. We discourage taking shots from the three-point range in order to conserve time. Each basket is worth one point. The shooter's partner should help count and rebound. You will need one basketball per set of partners.

5. **Crossing the gym:** Partners will run together at the same pace across the width of the gym space. You may choose to have them carry a track baton or plastic tube (12 inches long) and tap the opposite wall each time they cross over the running space. The partners will run 100 consecutive times across the gym space (most likely the width of a basketball court). You will need one baton per person.

6. **Scooter trips:** Partners can work at the same time. They will make 100 consecutive trips across a predetermined space (such as the width of a basketball court). Students may switch to a different travel method after 10 trips. Different travel methods may be repeated during the challenge. You will need one scooter per person.

7. **Frisbee catches:** Partners will throw a Frisbee back and forth until they each catch the Frisbee 100 times. If your gym space is small, we recommend that foam Frisbees be used for this challenge. You will need one Frisbee per set of partners.

8. **Jump rope:** Each partner will complete 100 consecutive jumps with a short jump rope. Partners may switch places after a miss occurs in order to give the jumper a short rest period. You will need one jump rope per set of partners.

9. **Soccer shooting:** Each set of partners will need a Nerf-type soccer ball and a folding tumbling mat. The partners will create a goal by standing the mat on edge and making it look similar to a hockey goal. Shooters will attempt to kick a goal from farther than a predetermined line on the floor (such as 15 feet). Each shooter will shoot 100 shots at the goal. You may or may not wish to use the other partner as a goalie. Partners could switch after every 10 shots on goal. You may choose to make the challenge 100 shots or 100 goals.

10. **Hockey shooting:** Using the same type of setup described in the soccer shooting challenge, and replacing the soccer-type ball with an indoor hockey stick and yarn ball, the partners will take either 100 shots at the goal or make 100 shots. Goalies are optional and turns may be rotated every 10 shots, if desired.

Competitive and Cooperative Features

Many of the activities you present in this challenge to your students will be self-motivating. The majority of students will be competing against the goal of 100 set up by the challenges themselves. There will also be a competitive desire to meet as many challenges as you present to the class.

There is a cooperative need to assist one's partner in achieving some of the challenges. There is a need for partners to encourage one another and to be supportive as each one attempts to achieve 100 successes in each event.

Safety Tips

1. Most of the activities described do not pose many safety concerns. However, spacing the students so they are not too close to other sets of partners is encouraged.
2. Whenever using scooters, instruction should be given concerning safe use of the equipment. No standing on them or using them as skateboards. Watch out for fingers by the wheels. Constantly watch for others and be respectful of their safety.

Teaching Tips

As previously mentioned, you may wish to give the students checklists or recording cards, or you may use a master list as a record.

There needs to be a commitment to honesty by the students. The possibility for recording false information is there. Discuss the use of an honor system and how partners serve as a help to that system.

Adaptations

We have listed 10 challenges that are easily administered in class. You, of course, can change the 10 challenges, or use as many challenges as you see fit. You may choose to provide an unlimited number of challenges for your students, but you may wish to give them a certain time limit in which they must complete the century challenges.

Special Comments

Again, we emphasize that you can create the activities to be used for Challenge of the Century. Ten is an easy number with which to work, but you can create any number of century challenges. Ten times 100 equals

1,000; therefore, you could rename this Challenge of the Millennium or put the name of your school in the title.

KICKING LESSON

Kicking Lesson was designed to be taught indoors, although it certainly can be done outdoors. We had found few activities, other than Kick Ball 300, that gave students adequate practice time kicking a rolled ball. Most kicking games do not allow many kicking turns for each individual student during the particular game. This lesson does require both a structure to the class period and a process for efficient movement in order to achieve the effectiveness intended.

Lesson Objectives

The skills of kicking and rolling a ball efficiently and effectively will be taught and reinforced during this lesson. It is expected that students will get many kicking turns and will be able to kick the ball relatively far.

Grade Range

This lesson can be taught at any grade level.

Activity Area

This lesson was created to be taught indoors, although it works well outdoors. You will want to use the largest space available indoors. Minimally, you will want an entire basketball court space. Outdoors, space is unlimited.

Equipment Needed

Class size and space may determine some equipment needs. You will need one base per group of three or four. For a class of 28, this would mean 6–9 bases. You will need at least one ball per group, but preferably about one ball per student. You may wish to use crash pads or tumbling mats to create a home run fence. Nerf or foam-type soccer balls are recommended for indoor kicking.

Activity Description

Depending on the size of your gym space, group the students so there is a minimum of three per group. You might have to put as many as five in a group. The groups each form a line at the center of the gym space or at least 25 feet from the kickers (see figure 5.19). One student per group sets a base in a line with the others, near a wall space at one end of the gym, facing their group. All group members except the person standing

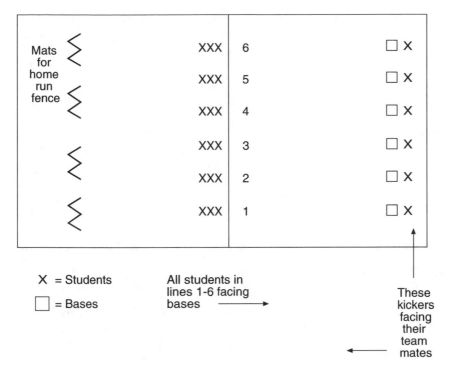

Figure 5.19   Kicking Lesson.

near the base will ideally receive a ball. However, you must have at least one ball per group. Use as many balls as possible. The groups need to have some type of numerical, alphabetical, or other named order. For the purposes of this explanation, we will use a number order.

If mats or crash pads are available, set up a home run fence a reasonable distance behind the numbered groups.

When first teaching this lesson, take time to teach the movement process. During the process, a number of students will be moving to different places at the same time. The first person in group one will pitch a rolled ball to the kicker in group one. The kicker will attempt to kick the ball as far as possible (hopefully over the home run fence). As soon as the first ball is kicked a few things take place. The kicker immediately chases the ball, retrieves it, and returns to line one (this may take a little time). The pitcher will begin to jog forward and go stand behind team one's base. The pitcher in line two will roll the ball toward kicker two, who will kick the ball and retrieve it. The pitcher from line two moves to take the kicking place at base two, and the pitcher in line three pitches the ball to kicker three. This process continues until each line pitches a ball. As soon as the last line (let's say line 6) pitches a ball and the kicker kicks it, group one begins the process again. Theoretically, only one ball at a time is being rolled. This assembly line of kickers will continue pitching, kicking, retrieving, and so forth, until you must stop them for instruction, encouragement, or other needs.

You will have ample opportunity to observe all students rolling the ball and kicking it.

Competitive and Cooperative Features

Unless you set up specific goals for performance (such as keeping track of home runs between groups or classes), the competitiveness seen in this activity usually is personal, in that students like to see how many home runs they can kick.

If classes demonstrate a high level of cooperation, there is constant pitching, kicking, and running taking place, resulting in a smoothly operating activity, with many kicking turns per student.

If there is a commitment to good pitching, there will be good kicking.

Safety Tips

1. Use a foam or Nerf-type ball indoors.
2. It is important that the pitchers do not pitch out of turn.
3. Teach the students to move quickly from pitcher to kicker position so that the student in the next line does not kick the ball into them when they are moving forward.
4. Students in the pitching line should always face the kickers so that if a kicker kicks a ball toward any individual, that person is able to catch the kicked ball, move away from it, or block the ball with the one he or she is holding.
5. Have students follow the flight of kicked balls. If a ball hits the ceiling, it may bounce directly onto another person.

Teaching Tips

1. Take time to teach the process for changing places. This will be one of the key elements to keeping the students working in a safe, efficient order.
2. Another key element for an effective lesson is for the pitchers to pitch well. The ball should be rolled straight, smoothly, and directly toward the base. Good pitching will ensure successful kicking.
3. We recommend that students receiving good pitches thank the pitcher for doing a good job. The politeness exhibited reinforces cooperation.

Adaptations

Adaptations are rarely needed in this lesson. Generally, the spacing of the group lines will require you to adapt the size of your groups, and the spacing will be determined by your teaching space.

STRIKING LESSON

Striking Lesson is a teacher-directed activity; that is to say, the teacher will be physically involved in this lesson to a very high degree. Like many of the other activities in this book, the lesson was designed to be taught indoors, although it can very easily be adapted to an outdoor space. For the purposes of the lesson description, we will make suggestions as they apply to an indoor lesson.

Lesson Objectives

The purpose of this lesson is to teach and reinforce the skill of hitting a pitched ball with a bat.

Grade Range

This activity is suitable for every grade.

Activity Area

You will need a large, open space such as a basketball court or gymnasium.

Equipment Needed

You will need approximately seven plastic bats (Whiffle ball bats), seven bases, which serve as home bases for the batters, and as many plastic balls (Whiffle balls) as possible (30–60 balls, or at least enough to fill up a box). Two containers, such as cardboard boxes, to contain the balls will also be needed. Additionally, you may wish to set up tumbling mats going across the gym, on edge, to serve as a home run fence. If you do this lesson outdoors, you will probably substitute the plastic equipment with softball equipment.

Activity Description

You will need to divide your class into four groups of relatively equal size. The four groups will each begin with a different task, but eventually rotate to participate in each of the four tasks.

Group one will start as the batting group. Group two begins as catchers. Group three starts as the teacher's (or pitcher's) helpers. Group four starts as the fielders. (See figure 5.20.)

The teacher will serve as the automatic pitching machine. The batters should be positioned in a slightly curved line, spaced far enough apart to prevent students from interfering with one another. The catchers will be positioned behind the batters, far enough away so as not to make contact with a bat. The helpers should be behind the pitcher (teacher). They are never to go in front of the pitcher while the pitcher is pitching.

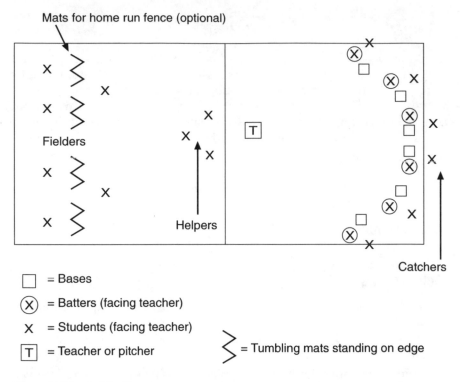

Figure 5.20   Striking Lesson.

Their task is to constantly fill the box provided them with balls. As soon as the pitcher empties a box of balls, the helpers bring the pitcher a new, filled box.

The fielders are positioned at the far end of the gym space. If you use a home run fence, some fielders will need to be on one side of the fence while other students are on the other side of the fence. It is the responsibility of both catchers and fielders to roll, not throw, the balls to the helpers. The pitcher begins by throwing an underhand pitch to the first batter. As soon as the first pitch is made, the pitcher pitches to the second student, and immediately the next pitch is given to the third student, and so on, until the last student in line is reached. The pitching order is then reversed. The last student, let's say student 7, receives another pitch (this means that the students on each end of the batting line will always get two pitches in a row after the first time through the line), then batter 6 receives a pitch, and the pitcher continues pitching to each batter to the end of the line. The process continues for about five minutes.

The batters are requested to try and hit each pitch given to them, even if the pitch is not perfect. If a pitch is particularly bad, that batter gets another pitch. As the batters are batting, some will miss the ball or hit a foul ball. The catchers are to roll any balls back to the helpers that go behind the batters. The helpers and fielders will be catching or retrieving batted balls hit out into the gym space. Fielders are also to roll the balls to the helpers. The helpers continually fill up the box (or boxes) not being held by the pitcher. Fielders also will try to catch as many fly balls as possible as well as try to rob the batters of possible home runs.

After about five minutes of batting, ask the students to stop and roll all balls on the floor to the helpers. When this has occurred, a rotation of positions will be requested. The batters lay down their bats and become the new fielders. The fielders rotate forward and become the new helpers. The helpers walk forward and become the new catchers. The catchers become the new batters.

The new rotation gets prepared and the automatic pitching machine begins again. Judge your time well enough so that each rotation of batters gets about the same amount of time to bat.

Competitive and Cooperative Features

Most students will want to hit the ball far and hit it often. There will be those who wish to hit as many home runs as possible. If you choose to make the activity a competitive one, we are sure you can come up with a number of competitive features: keeping track of individual hits and home runs, keeping track of group hits or home runs, giving the fielders points for catching various types of batted balls.

For this activity to be administered efficiently and effectively, a class needs to make a commitment to be cooperative. The more efficiently the students conduct themselves during each rotation and each of the four tasks, the more effective the pitcher will be. All this translates into more turns for individuals and more activity for the class.

Safety Tips

1. Batters must be safely spaced apart. Also, batters may never swing at any ball other than the pitch from the teacher. No ball should be golfed from the floor.
2. Catchers must be well behind the batters and never move forward into the batter's area.
3. Helpers must remain behind the pitcher while the pitcher is pitching. Never let the helpers go between the pitcher and batters. The helpers run the risk of getting hit by the pitcher's arm or a well-hit ball. The helpers should try to watch the batted balls as they are hit.
4. Fielders and catchers must roll the balls to the helpers. The helpers do not want to get hit by a thrown ball.
5. As the pitcher, you must use the box to make some of the world's greatest saves and also be prepared to catch or block batted balls hit toward you.

6. Always place all the left-handed batters on your left side. That will keep left-handed batters from hitting the right-handed batters on their follow-through.

Teaching Tips

1. Throw underhanded pitches. If you do not, accuracy may decline, plus your arm will wear out before the end of the school day.
2. Require strict adherence to the safety rules.
3. Once you have taught the rotation, you may wish to provide the fielding group with an additional assignment, such as an exercise or skill practice assignment. This will only be necessary if the fielders find themselves inactive or unchallenged.
4. Go over correct batting grip, foot position (stance), proper distance from home base, and terms such as choking up on the bat handle.

Special Comments

Depending on the height of your gym ceiling, you will have some balls taking unusual rebound bounces off the ceiling.

Have all students keep their eyes on the batters, not the fielders. This way most students will not get hit by a batted ball.

BIG BASE

There is a possibility that every school district has a game that bears some similarity to Big Base. However, once this game has been taught, we feel it has some features that will make this a favorite activity with your students.

Lesson Objectives

Big Base is a game that reinforces skills of kicking, pitching (rolling), catching, base running, and throwing and allows for a format of creating strategies within a game.

Grade Range

This game can be taught to students in grade 4 and above. The free-stealing part of the game should be taught in grades 6 and above.

Activity Area

Although this game will be discussed as an indoor game, it can be played outdoors. Look for comments in the adaptation section for changes to be made in playing outside.

Use a large gym space such as a basketball court. If you are fortunate to have a larger space, you can extend the distances between bases and make the playing area as large as possible. However, for this explanation, picture a basketball court as the size of the playing area.

Equipment Needed

You will need one Nerf-type soccer ball, one home base, four tumbling mats for bases, two sets of colored jerseys for team identification, and one scorecard (optional). We also recommend that four additional tumbling mats or crash pads be placed against the walls near each base to protect students from running into a wall space if the bases are placed near a wall.

Activity Description

Divide the students into two teams. Identify one team as the first kicking team and the other as the first fielding team. When teaching the game for the first time give each student on a team a number, starting with number one on each team to the highest number necessary, depending on your class size.

The fielding team should identify a pitcher, catcher, first, second, third, and fourth base person. All other fielders should play in an open area. The big bases (tumbling mats) should be opened and laid in the corners of the court, while the home base should be put an equal distance from bases four and one. Add the protection mats against wall spaces if needed (see figure 5.21).

Figure 5.21   Big Base.

There should be a central space identified as no one's land. No fielder may enter this area until the ball has been kicked on each kicking turn. This space can be a circle or rectangle—use existing floor lines in your gym space if possible, or use vinyl marking tape to make the shape.

The kicking team will be placed near home base, but out of bounds. We recommend that the people waiting their turns sit down so they are not mistaken as runners in the game by the fielding team.

You can use various methods to change pitchers, but we recommend a new pitcher each time there is a new kicker. As an example, player number one on the fielding team can pitch to kicker number one, fielder two pitches to kicker two, and so forth. You can also use various methods to change places in the field. For example, after a pitcher finishes a pitching turn, he or she could rotate to catcher. The catcher would become the first base person, first base person moves to second base, second to third, third to fourth, and the fourth base person becomes a random fielder.

Kicker number one will kick the ball into fair play and run to first base. Kicker one may advance to the furthest base possible. Once this person has stopped running, the next kicker will kick. Player number one does not have to run when kicker two kicks the ball (but may do so at his or her own risk). There are no limits on the number of people who can be on any given base. Runners may advance in any order as well or all at one time if desired. However, once a runner leaves a base, the runner must go on to the next base.

The fielding team will attempt to get the kicking team members out. The players can make outs in the following ways:

1. A fielder catches a fly ball.
2. A fielder tags a runner with the ball.
3. A fielder tags first base to force out the kicker (force-outs only occur at first base, not at any other base).
4. If a kicker kicks a foul ball, the person is out.
5. If a runner slides into any base, the person is out.
6. The fielding team players may throw the ball underhand only, to try and hit the runner. Any throw but an underhand throw means an automatic safe call for the runner.

When teaching Big Base, we recommend having all members of the kicking team kick before switching sides. Runners left on base at the end of an inning may return to that base the next inning. A run is scored when a kicker advances to all four bases and then tags home.

Unlike baseball, softball, and other kick ball games, runners do not have to tag up to advance on a fly ball that is caught. As we said, once a runner leaves a base (both feet step off the base) the runner must attempt to advance to the next base.

After the basic game has been taught, you may wish to play a certain number of outs per inning (such as five) and then switch tasks. Students always kick in their number order. If a person happens to be on base when his or her kicking turn occurs, the person may come to home base and take a kicking turn.

If you choose to keep score, place a scorecard conveniently near one end of the kicking line. A student puts a point on the scorecard when he or she scores a run.

For students in the sixth grade and above, you will want to advance to the free-stealing variation once the basic game is taught. In this variation, base runners may steal bases at any time, and there are no time-outs with the following exceptions. Runners may not advance if a foul ball is kicked or if a kicker misses a pitch.

Since the free-stealing variation changes the game so much, please be aware of the following changes:

1. Students do not stop at home but continue to first base and another trip around the bases.
2. Generally, students do not care to keep score, but rather find motivation in prolonging the team's kicking turn. Students can stay on base indefinitely.
3. You may wish to have pitchers pitch to three different kickers before rotating positions. Actually, when teaching this variation, it sometimes is best if the teacher does the pitching in order to set a very fast pace of pitching to kickers.
4. Five outs per inning usually is a satisfactory goal for each team. This number can be changed at your discretion.

Competitive and Cooperative Features

Attempting to advance on the bases, trying to score runs, and working to create outs all tend to create competitive aspects to the game.

Pitching well, working together on the base paths, and creating strategies for passing the ball all require cooperative skills.

The free-stealing variation of Big Base, without keeping score, invariably allows for a class atmosphere of great fun. The score means very little, and the fun of creating exciting spurts of running, risk taking, and daring base running takes precedence over who wins. The fun is in being on the base paths for as long as possible. The reward for good kicking and running skills is more kicking and running turns. The reward for good fielding skills is getting to switch back to the kicking turn more quickly.

Safety Tips

1. If big bases (tumbling mats) are placed near wall spaces, place protective mats or crash pads against the wall.
2. Do not allow catchers to block home base.

3. Fielders should leave a clear path between bases.
4. Do not allow sliding into bases.
5. Do not allow fielders to try and block kicks near home base.

Teaching Tips

1. Teach the basic game before teaching the free-stealing game.
2. Allow students to rotate fielding positions often.
3. Demonstrate what you expect for an underhand throw. Do not allow a student to throw a ball at another person with the intent of putting that person into orbit. This part of the game can be done safely in the spirit of fun.

Adaptations

If your gym space allows, create bonus point opportunities for kickers. As an example, if the variation is free stealing, the bonus could be circling the bases for a home run then receiving an additional kicking turn.

If you play Big Base outdoors, you can change the game to Super Big Base by placing the bases 100–200 feet apart. If you try this, consider having the students take two trips around the bases before they score a run and return to the kicking line for a brief rest. You may also wish to try using a soccer ball or playground ball when outdoors.

Special Comments

As in all games, allow your students to change or create rules that serve useful purposes for your class.

One key to the effectiveness of Big Base is getting the pitchers to pitch well and to pitch quickly to the next waiting kicker. A slow pitching process is discouraging.

KERHRIE

Kerhrie (pronounced Carry) is a running and kicking game originally adapted from an Indonesian game. It has evolved into a game that can be played indoors and outdoors. It is unlike most kick ball games in that there is quite a lot of running by both the kicking and fielding teams. Not everyone is guaranteed a kicking turn, but everyone will run.

This game is probably the hardest activity we have to explain. However, once the game is learned, the pattern of movement is not difficult to follow.

Lesson Objectives

This game includes the skills of running, dodging, changing directions, catching, kicking, throwing, rolling (pitching) a ball, and tagging.

Grade Range

This game is suitable for grades 4 and above.

Activity Area

You will need an indoor area at least the size of a basketball court.

Equipment Needed

You will need one foam or Nerf-type soccer ball, two sets of team jerseys to identify two teams, and three cones (preferably 18-inch cones, although you can make any size work). It will be helpful to make two lines (a goal line and a fielders line) with vinyl floor tape if you do not already have lines marked on the floor (see figure 5.22). A scorecard can be provided to keep score.

Activity Description

It may be helpful to explain the game in two parts. Part one is the kicking team's task and part two is the fielding team's role. For this explanation, we will use a basketball court to describe the playing area.

The basketball court is divided into a kickers half court and a fielders half court by a middle line called the fielders line. The fielding team spreads out in the area described as the fielders half court. A marking cone is set up near the middle line of the basketball court, about three to five feet into the fielders court. One fielder will pitch (roll) the ball to the first person on the kicking team who stands behind the goal line, which is located three to five feet from the back boundary of the kickers half court. After the kicker kicks the ball, the game

Figure 5.22   Kerhrie.

begins. There will be no foul balls in this game. However, if the kicked ball does not cross the center line, only the pitcher may run across the line to get the ball.

The kicking team will form a line near one corner of the kickers half court, outside the boundary of the playing court. The first kicker will stand near the center of the goal line to kick a pitched (rolled) ball. Once the ball is kicked, the kicker runs around the large cone and back across the goal line. The kicker may take any route to get around the large cone and may cross the goal line at any point between the two small cones that mark the ends of the goal line. If the kicker makes it back to the goal line, the person will score one point for the kicking team. Keep in mind, there is only one goal line in this game.

The next person in line does not kick the ball, but becomes the next runner and immediately runs around the large cone and back to the goal line. If the person makes it back safely, he or she scores a point, and the third person then takes off running. This process continues until an out is made. There is only one way to get a runner out. That is for the fielding team to get the ball, pass it to seven different people, then tag a runner with the ball.

Once an out occurs, play does not stop. The runner making the out stops running toward the goal line and chases the fielders across the same goal line. The runner will score one point for the kicking team for every fielder he or she tags. After everyone on the fielding team has crossed the goal line, the fielding team goes back to their half of the gym and a new pitcher rolls the ball to the next person in line on the kicking team. This process continues as described with the first kicker. You can set an arbitrary number of outs per inning. We suggest five outs the first inning. After five outs, have the teams switch positions.

It is helpful to number the kicking team members in order to keep their group in the same kicking order from inning to inning. Wherever they end one inning becomes their starting point the next inning.

Remember, there is only one way to create an out. Fly balls caught in the air do not create outs for the kicking team.

Now for the fielders role. No fielder may cross the fielders line until an out is made, with two exceptions. First, the pitcher may cross the line to retrieve the ball. Once the ball is picked up, the pitcher may throw it back to one of the other fielders, who begins the passing process. Second, if a fielder is chasing a runner, that person may cross the line to tag out the runner. As we said before, to create an out the fielders must pass the ball among seven different teammates. Each person must catch the ball. Each time the ball touches the floor, the passing must start again until seven different teammates make seven consecutive catches. The last person tags the runner with the ball to create the out.

As soon as an out occurs, the fielders attempt to run across the goal line. If one gets tagged by the runner on the kicking team, it means a point for the kicking team. After the fielders all cross the goal line, they return to their half of the court to start the next play with a new pitcher pitching. Always rotate a new pitcher for the next kicker.

Although we suggest playing five outs per inning, this number can be changed to meet any needs. If you only have a few minutes left in class, you might only play two or three outs the last inning in order to finish the game with both teams receiving the same number of turns by the conclusion of the class.

You might find it helpful to place a scorecard near the end of the kicking team's line. As each student returns to his or her team, the student adds the number of points he or she scored on the last turn to the scorecard.

Competitive and Cooperative Features

Scoring points, tagging runners, kicking for bonus points, and running fast all lend themselves to the competitive nature of the game. To reduce the competitiveness of the game, don't keep score. But elements of competition will still remain.

Pitchers need to pitch well so that kickers can kick well. Cooperating in this manner creates goodwill between teams and classmates. Fielders running across the goal line quickly in order to save time and start new turns add to positive feelings about the game. It is helpful to diminish the show-offy behavior of runners trying to lure the chaser into chasing them well after the rest of the teammates have crossed the goal line. Good passing results in more effective play as well.

Safety Tips

1. Do not allow the fielders to throw the ball at runners.
2. Do not allow runners to slide across the goal line.
3. It is possible that fielders might crowd around the large cone near the center (fielders) line. You might need to mark a semi-circle around that cone to keep it free from congestion.
4. Make sure that the goal line is set far enough from the end of the gym so that students do not run into the wall. You may need to set tumbling mats or crash pads against the wall to protect students.

Teaching Tips

1. Quite often you will have some students who attempt to be the seventh person to receive the pass from the fielding team. This person will then be the chaser. To avoid conflicts resulting from

this situation, require that the seventh person be a different person on each of the five out plays each inning.

2. Once the students understand the concept of the game, add the next seven to the seven–seven rule (that you are now creating). That is, the seventh person may only have possession of the ball for seven seconds. If the person has not tagged out the runner by then, he or she must pass the ball to another person. Keep in mind, if the ball is dropped or touches the floor in any manner before the runner is out, the fielding team must make seven more passes.

3. It is very likely that as you are teaching Kerhrie, the students will make a common mistake. Fielders will be tempted to cross the fielders line before the out is made. You must correct this behavior. The first time or two, point out the problem and use reminders. You might also try penalizing the fielding team one point per offender. You might give the kicking team an additional kicking turn. Please, however, get the students' attention on this situation.

4. There are times when runners like to show off and will not cross the goal line, but try to stay in the playing area in order to get the chaser to run after them. If this becomes a problem, require all fielders to cross the goal line within a specific time limit, such as five or 10 seconds.

5. There are times when a runner will go around the cone and then come back very slowly to the goal line. This situation sets up the next runner to get caught. Remind all the runners to run their fastest whenever they can.

Adaptations

You may need to experiment with distances between the goal line and fielders line as well as the best location for the cone that the runners will run around. The existing lines on your gym floor may or may not create the best distances.

Special Comments

Once Kerhrie is learned, the game will evolve according to your directions and teaching space. You may wish to add bonus points for certain types of kicking skills. Let's say a student kicks the ball and it hits the far wall in the gym, award a bonus point. If the ball hits a backboard, award five bonus points. Create numerous targets around your gym, it will result in risk taking. Many students are content to bunt or tap the ball rather than kick the ball toward the fielders.

WIDE GOAL SOCCER

Lesson Objectives

Wide goal soccer is a very active game that reinforces the skills of soccer dribbling, ball control, shooting, passing, and the two-handed overhead pass.

Grade Range

This game can be played at any grade level or by any age group.

Activity Area

This game is primarily an outdoor game, but could be played indoors if a large enough facility is available. A soccer field or football field would be a workable space. However, any area approximately 20–30 yards by 60 yards would work well (see figure 5. 23). A middle-of-the-field line will need to be provided.

Equipment Needed

You will need five or six soccer balls, two sets of team jerseys, and cones for marking boundary lines. You may provide a scorecard.

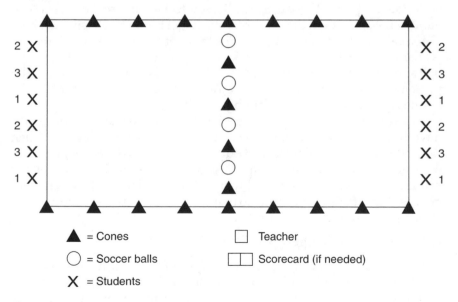

Figure 5.23   Wide Goal Soccer.

Activity Description

Each team will form a line across opposite ends of the playing field. Set the soccer balls spaced evenly apart along the middle line of the playing field. Players will need to be either numbered off by threes or put into three equal-sized groups for each team. The goals for this game will be the two end lines (the entire width of the playing field). For the purpose of explanation, we will number off the students 1, 2, 3, 1, 2, 3, and so forth, until all the students are numbered.

When you call out or signal the number ones to come out onto the field to play, the twos and threes will remain as goalies. The players on the field will attempt to get possession of a ball, dribble the ball the length of the field, shoot, and score a goal. Some students will dribble the ball unopposed, while others may have opponents attempting to defend them. If a student scores a goal, that person retrieves the ball, sets it down next to the teacher (who stands near the middle of the field at one side of the playing area), and reenters the game to either help a teammate, defend against an opponent, or score another goal with a different ball. Credit for a goal is given only if the ball is returned to the designated area.

If a ball is kicked over the heads of the goalies, no goal is scored. A goalie must then retrieve the ball, bring it to the goal line and throw it back into play using only the two-handed overhead pass (the type of pass a player in a soccer game would use if the ball goes out of bounds on a sideline play). If goalies are allowed to kick the ball or use a one-handed pass, the field players will simply get too tired chasing the ball.

If a ball goes out of bounds use the "rule of reason," that is, if no one is guarding you, bring the ball back into play and continue as though the ball was in play. If the ball goes out of bounds against a defender, the person not touching the ball last retrieves the ball, sets it down on the boundary line, and starts dribbling or passing.

After two minutes or when all the balls have been used to score goals, have the field players put the soccer balls back onto the center line. When they return to the goal lines, call out the number twos to play, with the ones and threes remaining on the goal lines as goalies. Repeat the process again with the threes playing while the ones and twos play as goalies. Adjust your time limits so that each group gets the same number of turns during the class period.

Competitive and Cooperative Features

This game can be played with a high degree of competitiveness. Players can display a lot of individual skill and desire. Players willing to do a lot of running can score multiple goals during a timed playing session. As the number of balls decreases during a playing turn, some aspects of team soccer can emerge.

In order for this game to be most effective, there must be a cooperative commitment by the players to adhere to certain rules such as the play of the goalies. If the goalies kick the ball into play rather than throw it into play, the game and the positive spirit of the game will break down. If goalies use a two-handed overhead pass to throw the ball into play, the distance they can throw the ball is limited. This limitation allows the field players an opportunity to get the ball back into an offensive direction quickly, and it limits the discouragement that can result if a player dribbles the ball a long distance, shoots, and then has to run all the way across the field to retrieve the ball again.

Again, a commitment to reasonable rules, such as use of hands or out-of-bounds play, helps to keep play constantly moving and reduces unnecessary discussions. More play equates with a better chance to use and develop skills in the game.

You could also make certain changes to allow for more teamwork such as requiring a pass to be completed before a goal is attempted.

Safety Tips

1. Goalies can be put into precarious positions if kickers get in close to them and kick their hardest. Request that students use good judgment when kicking goals, or set up a designated line away from the goal line that keeps kickers a certain distance away from the goalies.
2. Allow reasonable use of the hands, that is, if a student protects himself or herself from the ball with his or her hands, be understanding.
3. Goalies must remain on the end line or the goal line. They cannot come out on to the field to play the ball.

Special Behaviors to Observe

1. Goalies may not deliberately kick the ball into the field of play. They may use their hands or feet to block the ball or make a save. However, they may not kick the ball or use a one-handed throw to put the ball back into play.
2. Goalies often will come out too far from the goal line.

Teaching Tips

Once a goal is scored, the player scoring the goal must retrieve the ball and return it to you by running out of bounds and coming to the side of the field where you are standing. If you are using a scorecard, that would be the time for the player to add a point to his or her team's score. A player gets credit for the point when he or she sets (not throws) the ball down.

When a time limit comes to an end, have the players on the field help set the soccer balls on the center line in preparation for the next group.

This is one activity where you may need a whistle or some type of designated signal for students to hear from a distance.

Reinforce a set of reasonable rules such as the following: If hands are used but do not impact the direction of play, keep on playing. If hands are used to protect oneself from getting hurt, keep on playing. If hands are used to deliberately change the progress of another player, the ball automatically goes to the offended player.

Adaptations

The size of your field can be adjusted to the needs of your class. Also, the scoring system can be dramatically altered. You could give more points for scoring a goal using a certain colored ball. If you have soccer goals available, more points could be given for a ball kicked into the actual goal while still rewarding points for kicking across the end line. Additional points could be given if a ball is kicked through the uprights of a football goal post, if one is available. Points awarded could be determined in part by where on the field the ball was kicked. The scoring system could be changed by you or your students.

The number of soccer balls used can change some of the outcomes of the game. More soccer balls would add to more individual play, while fewer might require more team play.

ZONE PASSING

Lesson Objectives

The purpose of this game is to reinforce the skills of throwing, catching, centering (hiking), and running with a football. The game was originally intended to be an indoor game but can be played outdoors as well.

Grade Range

This game can be played from fifth grade through high school.

Activity Area

An area the size of a basketball court is needed for this game. If a larger area is available you can increase the number of teams or increase the number or sizes of the zones. For purposes of explanation, we will use an indoor basketball court to describe zone passing. See the section on adaptations for setting up outdoors.

Equipment Needed

For the purpose of this explanation, we will use three teams in our illustration. If your facility allows for more teams, you can simply add the necessary equipment.

You will need three air-filled, soft rubber footballs (one for each team). If possible, supply each team with a scorecard. You may also need some vinyl floor tape for marking lines.

We recommend soft footballs such as Itza or Poof balls because they have good texture and are more easily caught than foam-type balls. Older students may wish to use regular footballs, but keep in mind that softer balls allow for a high degree of success.

Activity Description

The first student in each line will start at the hiker's line (see figure 5.24). The second student on the team, the passer, will begin at the passing line. The first student centers (hikes) the ball to the passer and then runs to one of the three scoring zones. If the passer catches the centering pass, that team scores one point. The passer then throws the ball to the receiver (the person who centered the ball). Students catching the ball receive points based on the zone in which they make the catch. Zone one equals one point, zone two equals two points, and zone three equals three points. Whether the receiver catches or misses the pass, the receiver takes the ball, runs to the farthest wall, tags the wall, and runs the ball

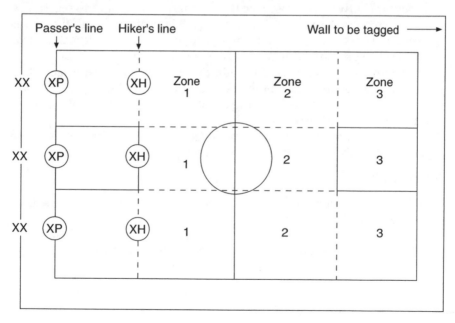

XP = Student passing

XH = Student hiking ball to passer. This student immediately becomes the pass receiver.

Figure 5.24   Zone Passing.

back to the passer. The passer will walk to the centering line while the receiver is running. The passer becomes the next hiker. The new hiker then hikes the ball to the next student, and the players repeat the process. Teammates can proceed as quickly as they can pass, run, and return the ball to the centering line.

Competitive and Cooperative Features

This game offers some very competitive opportunities as well as some wonderful cooperative situations. Students need to communicate to one another in order to go to the zones that allow for the most catching success. This also permits them to plan to take risks as well: If I am throwing to you, you may want to run farther away than I am capable of throwing. We need to decide what will work best for each of us. Of course, you can also encourage me to try to throw farther. If you are throwing to me and I am not confident of going to the farthest zone, your good passing and encouragement might allow me the opportunity to risk catching the ball farther away than I would normally attempt.

Teams usually will compare scores with other teams. To reduce competition between teams, give them goals or challenges to reach. The challenge may be for each team to exceed 30 points or for all the teams in combination to exceed 100 points. A challenge may be for each class to exceed the previous day's high score of, for example, 173 points.

One of the more desirable elements of this game is to teach each class to encourage teammates, whether successful or not. Recognizing good efforts or risks (such as attempting to catch the ball in the farthest zone) can be a continuous process.

The more efficient teams become in transferring the ball back to the centering line, the more passing turns they get during any time period.

Safety Tips

1. Students need to be careful about running into another team's zone or lane.
2. You need to take care that students do not run into a wall.
3. Do not allow a receiver to throw the ball back toward a team. The receivers may only run the ball back to the next person at the centering line.

Special Behaviors to Observe

1. Some students like to take risks. Sliding or diving in the gym could present safety problems.
2. Encourage recognition of good efforts, whether they are throws or catches.

3. Discuss methods of encouragement even when students make errors, miss the ball, or throw a poor pass.

Teaching Tips

1. You may wish to make tape numbers in each zone for teams to more easily identify scoring zones.
2. You may need to designate specific people to keep score (this task can be rotated).
   Examples: The person behind the passer can flip numbers, or the last person in line can tally the points, or as each person scores, they can add their points to the scorecard.
3. A receiver needs to tell the passer in which zone he or she feels comfortable trying to catch the ball.
4. Passers need to tell their receivers into which zone they feel they can throw the ball.
5. We suggest you use this game after teaching or reinforcing the skills needed in this game.

It does not serve a team well to throw the ball all the way into zone three if a student cannot catch the ball there. Conversely, if a student runs to the end of the gym, but the passer cannot throw the ball that far, it will be difficult to score points.

Adaptations

If a gym space allows for more teams or more zones to be created, take advantage of the situation and expand the opportunities.

This game can easily be played outdoors. If you do play outdoors, you can have teams of three or four players. You will need to have one ball and one scorecard for each team. You may wish to have one cone per team. Students could run around the cone rather than running to a wall or line. Outdoor space usually allows space for more zones (at least a four-point zone).

If your playground has sufficient grass, you can easily cut lines into the grass with a lawn mower set on a low setting.

Special Comments

If you play the game for more than 20 minutes, teams will likely score in excess of 100 points.

Many gymnasiums have objects such as climbing ropes, baskets, or cargo nets hanging from upper spaces. In fairness to all students, you may need to have teams rotate after a designated time to different throwing lanes so the obstacles do not interfere with only the same group of students.

TEAM HANDBALL

This version of team handball is a modified game. It is not the same game that is played in Olympic competition.

Lesson Objectives

This game combines elements of a number of competitive games. The skills of throwing and catching are the skills necessary for the greatest enjoyment and success in this game. Passing to teammates is not only desirable, but essential to the transfer of the ball and the creation of scoring chances.

Grade Range

This game is suitable for fifth grade through high school.

Activity Area

You will need a basketball court-sized area. Usually this game is played indoors but it could be played outdoors. If you have more than one basketball court available, you will be able to play with smaller teams and will not need to use the sideline players as described in the Activity Description.

You will need to provide a center line through the court (use existing basketball midcourt line) and a semicircle in front of each goal (see figure 5.25).

Equipment Needed

You will need one ball per court. The ball should be a firm foam ball, similar to a Nerf soccer ball. You may have to experiment to find the best

Figure 5.25 Team Handball.

ball possible. A seven-inch foam ball with good texture works well. Team members should wear a jersey to distinguish one team from the other. You will need to create a goal area for each team. One way to do this is to stand two tumbling mats on their ends, unfolded, to look like a large hockey goal or a small soccer goal. You may also choose to use a scorecard for the game.

Activity Description

For the purpose of the game description, we will assume you have only one basketball court with which you can work. Create two teams. Each team should wear colored jerseys. The teams will line up across the court from one another, behind the out-of-bounds line. If you wish, give each student a number, starting with number one on each team and continuing until each student has a number. The first three students from each team will come out onto the court and stand near the jump circle. These players will be designated as the offensive players (one center and two forwards). The next three students will come out and take the defensive positions (one goalie, two defenders).

The game begins with a jump ball, as you would to start a basketball game. As soon as the jump occurs, the offensive players must cross the center line. They will not be able to come back over the line during their turn. Conversely, the defensive players will not be able to cross the center line while they are on defense.

Offensive players may not enter the semicircular area in front of the goal. The goalie may not come out of the area within the semicircle. Defenders may travel throughout their entire half of the court.

During the course of play, players will attempt to work the ball close to the goal without crossing the semicircular line. Offensive players will try to throw the ball into the goal. The ball must hit the panels of the mats to count as a point (if you have nets available, use them).

Defensive players may attempt to intercept the ball or block the throwing attempt of the offensive players, but they may not touch the offensive players, nor may they take the ball away from them.

To keep the game moving quickly, all players must honor the three–three rule. That is, you may only take three steps when you have the ball, and you may only hold the ball for three seconds. Players without the ball may run anywhere within their boundary lines in an attempt to get better position for whatever strategies they try to employ.

If a goal is scored, the goalie immediately puts the ball back into play, the goalies only get three seconds to hold the ball just as all the other players do.

After a predetermined time (a few minutes), the players change positions. If you have one game going on, the offensive players rotate out of the game, the defensive players become offensive players, and three new defenders enter the game.

Begin the new time period with a jump ball or alternate throwing the ball into play as you would in a basketball game.

As the game is being played, the sideline players may be part of the action. Court players may throw the ball to one of their sideline teammates at any time. The sideline players may advance the ball down the line or throw it back to the court players. The sideline players may not score nor may they cross the boundary line to pick up a loose ball. They must also honor the three–three rule.

Anytime a ball crosses the side boundary line, the sideline players immediately put the ball into play. How you handle the end boundaries will depend on your facility. If there is a wall, place the goals near the ends of the gym and allow the throws that hit the walls to stay in play. If your facility is very large or you play out of doors, throws that go out of bounds immediately go to the opposite team (similar to soccer).

We recommend that goals only be counted when they come from direct throws, that is, if a ball hits a structural object, such as a basketball backboard, and rebounds into the goal, it would not count as a point.

Once this game is learned, the action is fast and furious. Players without the ball must get themselves to open spaces to receive a pass. Players must jump to catch passes or intercept them.

If your class has made a commitment to respecting the game and classmates, you usually do not have to create other rules. However, you might need to have some form of penalty if certain situations continue to cause problems in the game.

As we said earlier, defensive players may not steal the ball from offensive players (and vise versa). Sometimes, however, two players may simultaneously catch a ball or pick up a ball off the floor. You need to have a consistent pattern for this situation, such as the defenders get possession of the ball whenever this happens.

Competitive and Cooperative Features

There is a lot of fast action in this game. Scores sometimes reach very high numbers. Because of the quick changes going from offense to defense, the game can get very competitive.

For a team to be successful, there needs to be a lot of teamwork. Players must utilize good passes to one another. Moving while not having possession of the ball is sometimes more valuable than standing and waiting to catch the ball. Players who work to set up scoring opportunities for their teammates are very valuable assets to the team. Continually reinforce this particular resource.

Safety Tips

1. Players may not physically touch one another during the game.
2. Do not allow diving onto the floor.
3. Offensive players may not enter the semicircular area.

Teaching Tips

1. You might rule that attempted throws into the goal can only be overhand throws because this allows the goalies a better chance to predict the flight of the throw and be in a position to protect themselves as they make a save attempt.
2. When first learning the game, students might find the three–three rule hard to execute successfully. They will catch on after a few minutes of practicing the game.
3. Since goalie and center are two of the favorite positions, you might choose to have a system whereby a goalie cannot rotate to the center position on the next turn.
4. Students sometimes inadvertently cross over the center line. If it affects the play, the ball should go to the opposing team. If the crossing is of no consequence, let play continue.

Adaptations

If you have access to multiple courts, you can play five to eight a side (six seems to be the optimum number). Frankly, other than adjusting the numbers of players on each team and trying to incorporate sideline players into the game, we have not used adaptations to this game.

FRISBEE GOLF

Lesson Objective

Frisbee Golf has been around for a long time. It is a game of hand–eye coordination. If used without adaptations it is an enjoyable activity for any grade level, and, as a teacher, you can control the level of difficulty by the manner in which you create the course. By adding features of cooperation, teamwork, and running, you can emphasize different objectives.

Grade Range

This activity can be used from third grade through high school.

Activity Area

A large open field or playground will be needed. The area of a school campus could be used as well. To conduct the activity indoors, you would need a very large gymnasium or field house complex.

Equipment Needed

You will need one large cone or marker plus one hula hoop or tire for each hole (or target area) you set up (usually nine to eighteen).

Additionally, provide each student with a Frisbee. You may also wish to provide one pencil and note card per group or per person for keeping score.

Activity Description

The design of your course will take into account the available space with which you have to work. We recommend that you sketch out the course for reference and possibly mark the starting areas and holes with field spray paint for easy setup and multiple-day use.

Divide the class into groups of two to four. Each group can begin at a different numbered tee or starting area. Students can start by standing at the tee-off point and tossing the Frisbee toward their target hoop or tire (see figure 5. 26). After each group member completes a first throw, the group can advance for their second throw. Each group can throw in a specific order, or use golf etiquette to establish turns. Group members can record their scores at the end of each hole.

Competitive and Cooperative Features

Competing against a partner or small group is a very natural way of creating a competitive game. Comparing scores with other students in one's class or another class is easily done and certainly not unusual. Trying to improve your own score by throwing fewer times each round can slightly change the competitiveness to a personal challenge.

Cooperatively, partners could team together, share a Frisbee, and alternate throwing. The students could work together or in small groups to see how few times the Frisbee touches the ground while going from hole to hole; for example, the tee shot would have to be caught before the second shot is taken, and a penalty stroke is assessed if the Frisbee is not caught. Partners could alternate teeing off.

Safety Tips

There are few safety concerns with Frisbee Golf. You may wish to use golf etiquette terms such as "fore" if a Frisbee goes into the area of other players.

Teaching Tips

1. Students should be taught the correct grip for throwing the Frisbee.
2. Golf etiquette should be explained or discussed. Who throws first? When do you have the honors to begin?

Adaptations

1. Students could team together. One partner could throw to the other partner as the second person runs toward the hole and

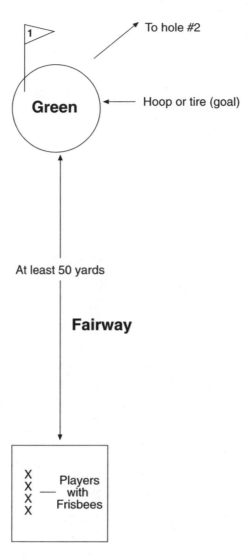

Figure 5.26   Frisbee Golf.

tries to catch the Frisbee. As soon as person one throws, he or she runs beyond person two in order to catch the next throw.

2. Students could be timed through the course. Speed could be combined with accuracy.
3. Allow groups of students to design a course periodically.
4. Partners could share a Frisbee and alternate throws.

APPENDIX

THE GREAT COMMUNICATOR

The Great Communicator is a very important challenge if you want to use the challenges to really build teamwork. Even though it is not a physical challenge like the others, it is essential for developing listening skills. If group members do not listen to one another, how can they communicate ideas? Group members also need practice speaking to one another so that they can clearly explain the ideas they wish to put into action. You can have all your groups try the Great Communicator at one time. Space is not an issue. This challenge can be done in a classroom or a gymnasium.

We suggest you try this challenge early in your team building program. As your groups develop (or struggle to develop), you may wish to repeat this challenge from time to time as a test of communication success.

Description

The group members sit either in a semicircle or randomly in an area assigned only to that group. One member of the group is selected as the Great Communicator.

The Great Communicator attempts to describe a picture in terms that will allow the group members to draw the objects being described. The Great Communicator may not, however, use certain terms describing standard shapes. Terms such as circle, square, rectangle, or triangle may not be used. Also, group members may not ask the Great Communicator questions or request further descriptions.

We suggest that you give the task of the Great Communicator to a different group member after each picture is completed.

Success Criteria

Unlike our other challenges, we have not defined criteria for success. The group members will show their group the completed pictures after the Great Communicator has completed his or her description. The group will be able to observe if they, as individuals or as an entire group, understood the descriptions given.

Equipment

Each group member will need a pencil and one piece of paper per drawing. You will need to give each Great Communicator a picture to describe (see the example drawings on the following pages or make up your own). A clipboard should be used by the Great Communicator so that the group members cannot see through the page he or she is using.

Setup

The only setup necessary is to give the group members the necessary equipment and to allocate a working space of a 10-foot circle or square for each group.

Rules and Sacrifices

There are no sacrifices for this task. The Great Communicator is not allowed to use the designated terms for shapes.

Possible Solutions

The solutions to this challenge will vary according to the descriptive skills of the Great Communicator and the listening skills of the group members. The purpose of this challenge is to give group members an opportunity to practice communication skills. As they display their drawings and compare them to the Great Communicator's picture, they will get an indication of their success in listening and speaking. As the group practices this challenge a few times, members should see an improvement in their communication efforts and skills.

Conclusion of the Task

The task is completed when the Great Communicator has finished describing the picture. The group members will show their finished drawings to the Great Communicator and to each other.

Additions and Variations

Feel free to use the picture examples we have provided on the following pages. As you use this challenge, you or your students can supply your groups with additional or more creative examples to describe.

Challenge Card — The Great Communicator

Equipment

Each group member will need a pencil and one piece of paper per drawing. The Great Communicator will be given a picture to describe and one clipboard on which to put the picture.

Starting Position

The group will sit in a semicircle or random space in front of the Great Communicator.

Our Challenge

Each group member will attempt to draw a picture from the description given by the Great Communicator.

Rules and Sacrifices

There are no sacrifices in this challenge. The Great Communicator is expected not to use the following terms: circle, square, rectangle, triangle, or certain other shape names. The group members may not ask the Great Communicator any questions.

The Great Communicator

Questions

1. What equipment do we use?
2. What is our starting position?
3. What can we ask the Great Communicator?
4. What terms must the Great Communicator avoid using?

Example 1   The Great Communicator

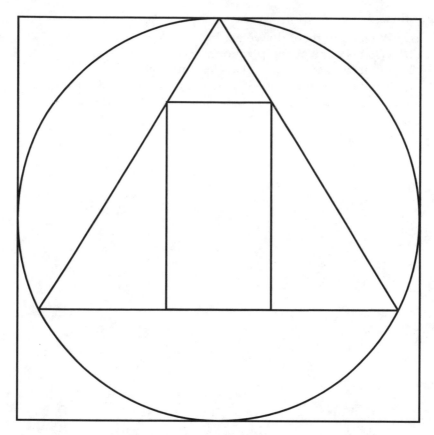

Describe this picture. You may not use the
following words:

Circle
Square
Triangle
Rectangle
Arc

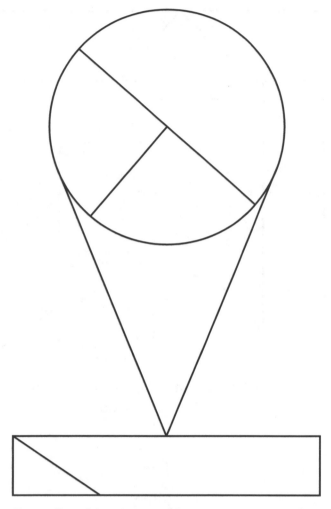

Describe this picture. You may not use the
following words:

Circle
Square
Triangle
Rectangle
Arc

Example 3 **The Great Communicator**

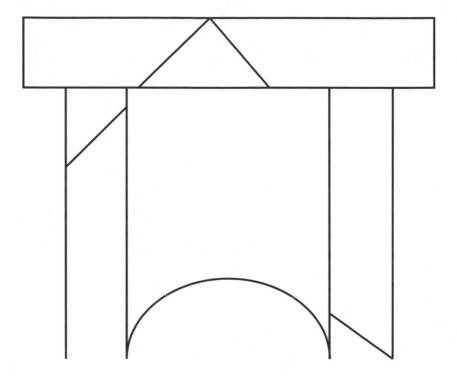

Describe this picture. You may not use the
following words:

Circle
Square
Triangle
Rectangle
Arc

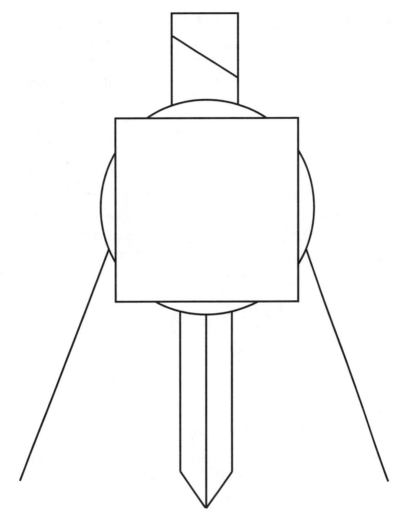

Describe this picture. You may not use the following words:

Circle
Square
Triangle
Rectangle

Pacing Lesson I Worksheet

Name _____ Class _____

	Goal	Actual			Goal	Actual
1.	15	_____ Lap time		1.	15	_____ Lap 1 time
				2.	30	_____ Lap 2 time

	Goal	Actual			Goal	Actual
1.	15	_____ Lap 1 time		1.	15	_____ Lap 1 time
2.	30	_____ Lap 2 time		2.	30	_____ Lap 2 time
3.	45	_____ Lap 3 time		3.	45	_____ Lap 3 time
				4.	60	_____ Lap 4 time

Set your own goal (12–18 seconds)

	Goal	Actual
1.	_____	_____
2.	_____	_____
3.	_____	_____
4.	_____	_____

Pacing Lesson II Worksheet

Name _____ Class _____

Warm up			Practice Lap		
Goal	**Actual**		**Goal**	**Actual**	
1. **15**	_____ Lap1 time		1.	_____ 1 Lap	_____ Lap time
2. **30**	_____ Lap 2 time				
3. **45**	_____ Lap 3 time				
4. **60**	_____ Lap 4 time				

Goal (seconds)	Actual time	2-Minute Jog		
		Goal (seconds)	Estimated laps	Actual laps
1. _____	_____	_____	_____	_____
2. _____	_____			
3. _____	_____			
4. _____	_____			

10-Lap Jog

Estimated lap speed	Estimated time running	Actual time
_____	_____	_____

Fitness Decathlon Sample Student Evaluation

Name _____ Class _____

Fitness challenge	Number of completed repetitions	Points
1. Curl-Ups	1. 2.	Add both scores
2. 10-Minute Run	time:	
3. Shuttle Run	time:	
4. Rope Jumping (long rope)	jumps:	
5. Bent Arm Hang	seconds:	
6. Push-Ups	number completed:	
7. Jumping Jacks	number completed:	
8. Pull-Ups or Chin-Ups	number completed:	
9. Rope Jumping (short rope)	jumps:	
10. Sit and Reach (flexibility test)	inches or centimeters:	

Challenge of the Century
Sample Student Evaluation

| Name _____ | Class _____ |

Challenge	Points Scored		
	1st Attempt	**2nd Attempt**	**3rd Attempt**
1. Throw and One Bounce Catch			
2. Partner Toss and Catch			
3. Baseball or Tennis Ball Throw and Catch			
4. Basket Shooting			
5. Crossing the Gym			
6. Scooter Trips			
7. Frisbee Catches			
8. Jump Rope			
9. Soccer Shooting			
10. Hockey Shooting			
Total Points Accumulated			

My favorite challenge was _____

My most difficult challenge was _____

My partner was _____

Team Report Card

1. How did our team involve everyone in solving the challenge?
2. Did our team use negative pressure or put-downs during the challenge?
3. Did we listen to one another and use ideas that we shared?
4. How many and which team members used praise phrases or positive encouragement?
5. What were some of the praise phrases used?

BIBLIOGRAPHY

Anderson, Leigh. 1996. "Incorporating teamwork into competitive situations." Master's thesis, Hamline University.

Ferguson, Howard E. 1983. *The Edge*. Cleveland, OH: Getting the Edge Company.

Glover, Donald and Midura, Daniel. 1992. *Team building through physical challenges*. Champaign, IL: Human Kinetics.

Grineski, Steve. 1996. *Cooperative learning in physical education*. Champaign, IL: Human Kinetics.

Kohn, Alfie. 1986. *No contest*. New York: Houghton Mifflin.

Luvmour, Sambhava. 1990. *Everyone wins*. Philadelphia: New Publishers Society.

Martens, Rainer. 1977. *Competition: Misunderstood and maligned*. Champaign, IL: Human Kinetics.

McNally, David. 1980. *Even Eagles Need a Push*. Transform Press.

Midura, Daniel and Glover, Donald. 1995. *More team building challenges*. Champaign, IL: Human Kinetics.

Nelson, Mariah Burton. 1991. *Are we winning yet?* New York: Random House.

Oglesby, Carol. 1978. *Women in sport: From myth to reality*. Philadelphia: Leafrebiger.

Orlick, Terry. 1978. *Cooperative sports and games book*. New York: Pantheon Books.

Orlick, Terry. 1982. *The second cooperative sports and games book*. New York: Pantheon Books.

Ralbovosky, Martin. 1974. *Lords of the lockerroom*. New York: P.H. Wyden.

Runfola, Ross and Sabo, Donald. 1980. *Jock: Sports and male identity*. Englewood Cliffs, NJ: Prentice Hall.

Sherif, Carolyn. 1976. *Social problems in athletics*. Champaign, IL: University of Illinois Press.

Torbert, Marianne. 1980. *Follow me: A handbook of movement activities for children*. Englewood, NJ: Prentice Hall.

U.S. Department of Health and Human Services. 1996. *Physical activity and health: A report of the Surgeon General*. Atlanta, GA: U.S. Department of Health and Human Services, Center for Disease Control and Prevention, National Center for Chronic Disease Prevention and Health Promotion.

ABOUT THE AUTHORS

The Midura Family
Luke, Shirley, Dan, and Seth

The Glover Family
Back row: Christina, Bruce, Matt, Mark, and Leigh. *Middle row:* Don and Jessie. *Front:* Carol, Alexa, and baby Jacob.

Dan Midura has taught physical education since 1970. He is the elementary physical education coordinator for the Roseville, Minnesota Area School District. He is active in several professional organizations, such as the Minnesota Association of Health, Physical Education, Recreation and Dance (MAHPERD); the American Alliance for Health, Physical Education, Recreation and Dance (AAHPERD); the Council on Physical Education for Children (COPEC); and the National Association for Sport and Physical Education (NASPE). A former president of MAHPERD's Physical Education Council, he was elected the 1998-99 president of MAHPERD.

Midura has received many awards over the course of his career, including MAHPERD's 1995 Paul Schmidt Award, Minnesota's highest honor to physical education and health educators. Midura earned his master's degree in physical education from the University of Minnesota in 1977.

Don Glover has taught physical education, including adapted physical education, since 1967 at the preschool, elementary, secondary, and postsecondary levels. He currently teaches adapted physical education in the White Bear Lake (Minnesota) School District.

In 1981 Glover was recognized as Minnesota's Teacher of the Year and was named the Minnesota Adapted Physical Education Teacher of the Year in 1989. He earned his master's degree in physical education from Winona State University in 1970. A past president of MAHPERD, he is also a member of AAHPERD, NASPE, COPEC, and the Minnesota Education Association.

Together, Midura and Glover wrote *Team Building Through Physical Challenges* (Human Kinetics, 1992) and *More Team Building Challenges* (Human Kinetics, 1995). If you are interested in a team building workshop for your school district, company, or state or regional conference, contact Don Glover at 612-779-6904 or Dan Midura at 612-553-1374.